WALKING ANGLESEY'S SHORELINE

Walking Anglesey's Shoreline

by DAFYDD MEIRION

First published 2003

© Text and photographs: Dafydd Meirion

Copyright © by Gwasg Carreg Gwalch 2003.
All rights reserved. No part of this publication may be reproduced
or transmitted, in any form or by any means, without permission.

ISBN: 0-86381-827-7

Cover design: Sian Parri/Alan Jones

Published by
Gwasg Carreg Gwalch,
12 Iard yr Orsaf, Llanrwst,
Wales LL26 0EH
✆ 01492 642031   📠 01492 641502
✆ books@carreg-gwalch.co.uk
Internet: www.carreg-gwalch.co.uk

The author nor the publishers takes any responsibility
if you are injured or if you – against advice given –
are caught trespassing.

Dafydd Meirion

A journalist from Dyffryn Nantlle near Caernarfon.
Has published two novels, *Pî-Âr* and *Trôns*, and *Cymry Gwyllt
y Gorllewin*, the history of the Welsh in the American Wild
West. His hobbies are walking, history and writing which have
all come together to produce this book.

*Cyflwynedig i
Myrddin ac Eleri
er cof am y teithiau pleserus ym mynyddoedd Eryri
a sawl peint ar ffordd adref*

5 miles

5 km

Introduction

Ynys Môn (the Island of Anglesey), once an island of inhospitable forests and wild, rocky coasts, the land of the Druids is now a tourist destination, served by the North Wales Expressway from England and the fast ferries from Ireland.

It became separated from the mainland at the end of the last Ice Age (about 5,000BC) when retreating glaciers melted and flooded a valley that became Afon Menai (the Menai Strait). But the first visitors came here during prehistoric times, before the flooding. The excavation of a headland site at Aberffraw revealed vast quantities of flint from around 6000BC, the Mesolithic (Middle Stone Age) era. These people were hunters but were followed around 3500BC by the Neolithic (New Stone Age) people who practised agriculture. They cleared woodland for fields and built stone tombs for their dead, such as at Barclodiad y Gawres, Bodowyr and Lligwy.

The next wave of people came during the Bronze Age (1600BC) and introduced metal working to the island. It is thought that copper was first mined on Mynydd Parys during this period. Round barrows, standing stones and stone circles are testimony to their presence.

Celtic tribes from Europe moved into Britain during the 6th century BC (the Iron Age). Farmsteads and hillforts such as Dinas Gynfor and Caer y Tŵr were established during this time.

When the Romans came here first in AD61, the island was an important centre for the Druids. In a major battle, the unarmed Druids were slaughtered and their sacred oak groves destroyed. The island was ruled from the Roman fort at Segontium (Caernarfon) on the mainland although a fort and naval base was established at Caergybi (Holyhead).

During the 5th and 6th centuries, Christian missionaries reached the island and founded churches and monasteries such as at Caergybi and Penmon. Many of these missionaries came to be known as saints and are commemorated in numerous churches and holy wells, such as Saint Seiriol and Saint Gwenfaen. It was at around this time a royal court was founded at Aberffraw and it became a centre of culture and administration.

But the next visitors were not so friendly. From the 9th century onwards, Vikings from Ireland and the Isle of Man attacked the island. In 961 and 967 the monasteries came under attack and in 968 the palace at Aberffraw was partly destroyed. The Vikings did not settle here but many of the names of the islands such as Skerries and Priestholm (and possibly Anglesey) are testimony to their presence.

The Normans, led by the Earl of Chester, invaded the island in 1090 and built a motte and bailey castle at Aber Lleiniog near Llangoed. Four years later it was captured by Gruffudd ap Cynan and, with the end of the Viking raids, this period became a prosperous one when stone churches, such as Penmon and Capel Lligwy, were built. At this time, the trees were cleared and the island became a fertile land where huge quantities of grain were grown. The saying Môn Mam Cymru (Anglesey, Mother of Wales) came into being as it supplied large areas of the mainland with food.

This was a period when Wales was ruled by the native Welsh princes such as Llywelyn Fawr (Llywelyn ap Iorwerth or Llywelyn the Great) who took the title Prince of Aberffraw and Lord of Snowdon. His wife Siwan, daughter of King John of England, was buried at the Franciscan friary at Llanfaes near Beaumaris. After his death, his grandson Llywelyn ap Gruffudd (ein Llyw Olaf – the Last) ruled most of Wales and during the wars of 1276-7 and 1282 with England, Edward I seized Ynys Môn's corn harvest to weaken the resolve of the Welsh. The death of Llywelyn in 1282 at Cilmeri in mid Wales brought an end to Welsh independence and Anglesey became a county in 1284 under the new English rule. In order to stop further revolts a ring of castles were built around Wales with work on

Beaumaris castle beginning in 1295. But in 1402 Owain Glyndwr captured the castle and held it for two years.

In 1485 Henry Tudur (or Tudor) whose family came from Penmynydd on the island defeated Richard III at Bosworth and he became Henry VII, the first Tudor monarch.

Industrialisation came to the island during the 18th century when copper was mined on a vast scale on Mynydd Parys and the small port of Amlwch expanded in order to export the ore. Another product was limestone which was quarried on the eastern side of the island and exported from various ports. Agriculture remained important and numerous windmills were built across the island to grind the corn. Fishing was also important and there were numerous fishing villages dotted along the coast where the fish was landed, sometimes cured and then sold across the island or even exported.

Once the Menai Strait had been formed, people had either to cross to the island by boat or cross the treacherous Traeth Lafan by foot. From the Middle Ages onwards ferries carried people to and from the mainland, and from the 17th century onwards packet boats began sailing to Ireland. During the early 19th century, the government in London was keen to have a quick, safe route to Ireland and Thomas Telford was commissioned to construct the Holyhead Turnpike Road (later the A5) to Caergybi, and Pont y Borth (the Menai Suspension Bridge) was built in 1828. By 1850, Robert Stephenson's Britannia Bridge across the Strait had been built and it was possible to travel by train from London to Caergybi, which became an important port for the ferries to Ireland. Anglesey was also near the busy shipping routes to Liverpool and numerous lighthouses and lifeboat stations were built to try and avoid loss of life in the numerous shipwrecks.

From the beginning of the 20th century, tourists began to arrive on the island and small fishing villages such as Trearddur, Rhosneigr and Benllech developed into holiday resorts. Today, tourism is a major employer although agriculture is still important. Many are employed at the aluminium works in Caergybi and at Wylfa power station on the north coast as well as on industrial parks at Llangefni and Caergybi.

Places of historical interest are printed in **bold** with details included at the end of each walk. These are only short notes and a list of books that will give you more information is at the back of this book.

YNYS MÔN

The Welsh have always called the island Ynys (island of) Môn and the Romans referred to it by its Brythonic (the forerunner of the Welsh language) name, Mona. But the Vikings called it Anglesey – the island in the strait, some say; others from Ondull's Eye after a Viking chieftain who invaded the island. Another explanation offered is that the Saxon King Egbert who invaded the island in 853 named it Angle's Ey (Isle of the Angles).

WALKING

If you are used to walking you might like to attempt to walk around the island in one go – you should be able to do the 130 miles in between six and ten days. You can combine some of the routes to give you a good day's walking. There are plenty of camping sites, inns, hotels, B&Bs along the coast, but no youth hostels. During the summer season it is advisable to book in advance. For more information look up the websites
http://www.visitanglesey.com/
http://www.anglesey.gov.uk/english/tourism/home.htm
http://www.walestouristsonline.co.uk/anglesey/index.html

On the other hand you may wish to do the walks bit by bit. The ideal would be to walk with a companion so that you can leave one car at your destination before starting off, saving you having to walk back. There are also local bus routes along many of these journeys which you can use to return to your car. I have not published times as these can vary; leaflets with the latest times can be found in various tourist information offices or by looking at Ynys Môn Council's website www.anglesey.gov.uk, look under the Tourism and Leisure section, Anglesey Bus Journey Planner.

Also included are circular routes which take you along the coast but offer a return journey inland.

You are allowed to walk between high water mark and low water mark but this is not always possible as a number of small harbours have been built. If you want to cross private property (or what looks like private property) please ask for permission.

Since a lot of the walking involves going along the shore, please check the tides. Booklets are available in local shops but you can also check the website http://www.pol.ac.uk/home/tides/. It is much easier if you can do most of the walks when the tide is out as it means you can walk on sand rather than clambering over rocks.

Ynys Môn is noted for its abundant wildlife. Be especially careful during the nesting season – April/May – and when you see signs warning you, please keep away.

Apart from the shore, all the routes cross private land, even though they are designated as footpaths. Keep well away from any livestock and crops and try to cross fields by their edges unless there is a properly defined path.

Some of these walks involve walking along clifftops. Be very careful if you have children with you. Some of the more difficult parts are not suitable for children or dogs.

The times and miles given are only approximate as it depends what route you take – footpaths or clambering over rocks. It also depends how fast a walker you are (I was constantly stopping to make notes and take photographs). Take your time, and take in the wonderful views.

WHAT TO WEAR
It is advisable to wear walking boots for these walks and if you want to avoid blisters two thick pairs of socks. Although it

depends what time of year that you do the walks, it is always advisable to take warm clothes with you, even on a sunny summer day as the wind can often be very cold. It is preferable to have layers of clothing that you can take off as you warm up. If you are walking in cold weather, it is also advisable to take a warm, woolly hat and gloves.

You will be very fortunate if you do not encounter any rain. Take with you wet weather clothing, including trousers. If you intend staying overnight along the way, take some spare clothing with you.

Two 1:25,000 OS maps (Explorer 262 and Explorer 263) will cover the island for you. Always take them with you, along with a compass, because although you are not very far from civilisation there is the slight chance that you will be caught in some sea mist.

ADVICE

Readers are advised that whilst every effort is taken by the author to ensure the accuracy of this guidebook, changes can occur which may affect the contents. It is advisable to check details locally before and during each walk.

Some of these routes can be difficult and the advice is not to take small children with you or dogs (which may be prohibited from some beaches anyway and may worry farm animals) unless stated that it is a safe stretch of beach. Even adults and older children should be very careful in some places.

THE COUNTRY CODE

Guard against any risk of fire

Keep to the public rights of way when crossing farmland

Avoid causing any damage to walls, fences and hedges

Leave farm gates as you find them

Keep dogs under control and on leads in the presence of livestock

Leave machinery, farm animals and crops alone

Take care not to pollute water
Carry your litter home with you
Protect all wildlife, plants and trees
Avoid making any unnecessary noise
Drive carefully on country roads
Enjoy and respect the countryside

PLACE NAMES

Very few place names on Ynys Môn have an English equivalent. When there are, these are given in brackets. To help you understand what some of these place names mean, here is a list of Welsh words. They are often followed by the names of saint or princes or topographical features, e.g. Llangefni – church on the river Cefni.

Aber – *estuary, river mouth*
Afon – *river*
Allt (Gallt) – *slope*
Bach (Fach) – *small*
Barcud – *kite*
Bedd – *grave*
Bron – *breast of a hill*
Bryn – *hill*
Bwlch – *pass*
Cae – *field*
Caer – *fort*
Capel – *chapel*
Carn – *cairn*
Carreg – *rock, stone*
Castell – *castle*
Coch – *red*
Coed – *wood*
Cors (Gors) – *bog, marsh*
Craig – *rock*
Croes – *cross*
Cromlech – *burial chamber*

Cwm – *valley*
Dinas – *fort*
Dôl/Ddôl – *meadow*
Du/Ddu – *black*
Dŵr – *water*
Dyffryn – *valley*
Eglwys – *church*
Ffordd – *road*
Ffynnon – *spring, well*
Gefail (Efail) – *smithy*
Glan – *river bank*
Glas – *blue, green*
Gwyn – *white*
Gwynt – *wind*
Hafod – *summer dwelling*
Hen – *old*
Hendre – *winter dwelling*
Heulog – *sunny*
Hir – *long*
Isaf – *lower*
Llan – *church*
Llyn – *lake*
Llys – *court, palace*
Maen – *stone*
Maes – *field*
Mawr (Fawr) – *big, great, large*
Melin – *mill*
Moel (Foel) – *bare hill*
Morfa – *sea marsh*
Mynachdy – *monastery*
Mynydd – *mountain*
Nant – *stream*
Newydd – *new*
Ogof – *cave*
Pant – *hollow*

Parc – *park, field*
Pen – *head, top*
Penrhyn – *promontory, headland*
Pentir – *headland*
Pentre – *village*
Plas – *mansion*
Pont – *bridge*
Porth – *port, entrance*
Pwll – *pool*
Rhos – *moorland*
Rhyd – *ford*
Tafarn – *inn*
Traeth – *beach*
Tref – *town*
Trwyn – *promontory*
Twr – *tower*
Tŷ – *house*
Tyddyn – *small farm, smallholding*
Uchaf – *upper*
Y (Yr) – *the*
Ynys – *island*

And if you want to greet someone in Welsh –
Bore da – *good morning*
Pnawn da – *good afternoon*
Noswaith dda – *good evening*
Os gwelwch yn dda – *please*
Diolch – *thank you*

The Routes

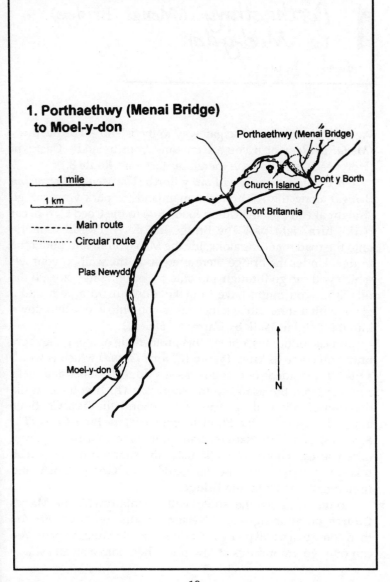

1. Porthaethwy (Menai Bridge) to Moel-y-don

1 mile

1 km

- - - - - - - Main route

·············· Circular route

Porthaethwy (Menai Bridge)

Church Island

Pont y Borth

Pont Britannia

Plas Newydd

Moel-y-don

N

1 Porthaethwy (Menai Bridge) to Moel-y-don

7 miles – 2 hours

We start our walks at the gateway to the island – **Porthaethwy** *(Menai Bridge)*, or if you are crossing from Ireland – Caergybi (Holyhead), and you can therefore start with Route 8.

Once you have crossed **Pont y Borth** *(The Menai Suspension Bridge)* along the A5 from the mainland (to park your car, go straight ahead past the Co-op food store to the Coed Cyrnol car park), turn right past The Bridge Inn down Ffordd Cambria onto the road that runs alongside the Menai Strait and under the bridge. Under the bridge there is a gap in the wall on your left which you can go through and onto rocks along the shore. If the tide is in, you might have to make a detour up a path into a glade with a stone circle which takes you onto a lane and down into the **Belgian Walk** by Carreg yr Halen.

You can either walk along this promenade or along the shore until you come to **Ynys Tysilio** *(Church Island)* which is worth a visit. If the tide is out, you will see a ridge of stones and rocks running from the island to the shore on which you can walk. Otherwise, you will have to walk around the bay. Continue along the shore, in the Strait to your left are **Pwll Ceris** *(The Swellies)* and **The Platters**, until you come to a bench. From here you can choose to walk along the shore or a path which takes you past Ynys Benlas and **Ynys Gorad Goch** and underneath the **Britannia Bridge**.

Continue along the shore with Llanfairpwll's **St Mary's Church** on your right and **Nelson's Statue** on your left. You then come to a small pier with a round, white building on it. You can only go around this at low tide. Then onto a small estuary at **Y Felin Heli**. Cross the river and go along the shore to **Pwllfanog**. From here, there is a path on National Trust land running alongside the shore for some distance before turning inland into woodland*.

Follow the shore until you come to **Plas Newydd** and its huge sea wall and docks. You can only walk around them at low tide, and even then you might have to wade in the water. If this is not possible, my suggestion is to walk along the path through the woodland (see above*) which is on Plas Newydd land towards the main gate. Pay the admission price which allows you to wander around and then walk to the front of the mansion. Bear right and go to the far end of the docks where you will see some small stone steps by a hut which go up and then down to the shore.

If the tide is in, you will come across a couple of lagoons which you will have to be very careful in going around them as they have steep sides. On the opposite side of the Strait, in their various pastel colours, are the houses of Y Felinheli Marina, and then opposite **Moel-y-don** Y Felinheli itself. When you reach Moel-y-don, you will see an embankment running from the shore with a white house at its end. Walk along the shore alongside this roadway until you come to the Pilot's Cottage and then onto the road and the end of the first stage.

Parts of this route are very difficult especially if the tide is in and you may prefer an easier route. Park in the **Coed Cyrnol** car park near the Co-op store after going over the suspension bridge and follow the main road (there is a pavement to walk on) until you see the **Marquis Column** on your right; then turn left down the A4080. If you are feeling energetic, you may wish to climb the column (115 steps). Also nearby is an old turnpike house, built at the same time as the A5. Further along is the Women's Institute building; it was here that the first Women's Institute branch was established in Britain.

Keep on this road for two miles, passing **Plas Newydd**. Then turn left down a road signposted **Moel-y-don**. Pass the entrance to **Plas Coch** Caravan and Camping site on your right and on your left the entrance to **Llanedwen Parish Church** and down to the shore at **Moel-y-Don**.

CIRCULAR ROUTE
3 miles – 1 hour

Park in the Coed Cyrnol car park near the Co-op store after going over the suspension bridge. Out of the car park, turn left and cross the road towards St Mary's Church. Into the church grounds and on reaching the church you will see a path with handrail leading down through some trees. Follow the path and you will reach the main road through Porthaethwy (Menai Bridge). Then left and follow the road through the town until you see Ffordd Cadnant. Up this lane which takes you near the shore at Cadfan Villa.

*Turn right to follow **Ffordd Cynan** which runs parallel to the shore until you come to a timber yard. Follow Lôn Cei Bach (Beach Road), past Porth y Wrach and under Pont y Borth (The Menai Suspension Bridge). Follow the path on your left through trees where there is a stone circle. Back onto the road and down to the Belgian Walk.*

Along this promenade to the embankment, cross to Ynys Tysilio (Church Island) and walk clockwise around the island visiting the ancient Church of St Tysilio which is sometimes open, past Cynan's grave and back to the church gate. Then up the hill through Coed Cyrnol until you arrive back at the car park where you started.

PLACES OF INTEREST
A5: This was the original post road from London to Caergybi (Holyhead) via Chester. By 1660, there was a regular postal service to Caergybi. It became a turnpike road following various acts of Parliament during the 1750s and 1760s. It has been superseded as the main route to Ireland by the opening of the A55 Expressway which was opened in the 1990s and extended

across Ynys Môn in 2000.

Belgian Walk: A waterside promenade built by Belgian refugees during the First World War. It was repaired in the 1960s after storm damage and reopened in 1965 by the only member of the group still alive, Monsieur Eduard Willems.

Britannia Bridge – was built by Robert Stephenson in 1850 to carry trains through two wrought-iron tubes to Caergybi (Holyhead). It burned down in 1970 leaving only the limestone piers. When it was rebuilt, an additional deck was placed on top to carry road traffic (the present A55).

Coed Cyrnol – is situated on a rocky promontory called Cerrig y Borth. It was once common land, traversed by numerous paths for the inhabitants of Porthaethwy to reach the causeway leading to Saint Tysilio's Church. Yn 1814, the Earl of Uxbridge (later the Marquis of Anglesey) took over the promontory and planted trees. The area became known as Coed Cyrnol (the Colonel's woodland) after a certain Colonel Sandys that lived nearby at the end of the 19th century.

Church of Saint Mary, Llanfairpwll: The original church was medieval, but was rebuilt in 1853. There is a stone memorial here to the eighteen who died during the construction of the Britannia Bridge.

Church of Saint Tysilio: Founded by St Tysilio (son of Powys king Brochfael Ysgythrog) around 630AD on Ynys Tysilio (Church Island). On the island is a war memorial in the form of a Celtic cross.

Ffordd Cynan: Named after well-known poet and archdruid Cynan. He lived in the town for many years and is buried on Ynys Tysilio (Church Island).

HMS Conway: In 1953 the old sail warship *The Nile* with 92 guns was destroyed on the Platters rocks. At the time she was a sail training ship – the *HMS Conway*. Her back was broken as she tried to run with the tide on her way to Liverpool to be refitted.

Llanedwen Parish Church: Saint Edwen is believed to have founded a cell here in 640AD. The church was almost completely rebuilt in 1856; the remains of the earlier church is to be seen in the lower part of the west wall. Some of the gravestones and church furnishings date from the 15th and 17th centuries. This church is probably the only church in Wales in regular use to be lit entirely by candles. Some of the earlier members of the Plas Newydd family and their retainers are buried here.

Marquis Column: It was built in 1816 to commemorate The Marquess of Anglesey's bravery in the Battle of Waterloo. The statue on the top was added 43 years later, a few years after the Marquess died. It is possible to walk inside the column, up its 115 steps, to the top giving magnificent views of Ynys Môn.

Moel-y-don: Ferries ran from Moel-y-don to the mainland at Y Felinheli from about 1400 to 1850 when the Menai Bridge was built. Ships of over one hundred tons were built here towards the end of the 18th century.

At one time there was a slate plaque at Y Felinheli, on the opposite side, commemorating a battle here in 1282 between the army of Edward I and the Welsh. The English king had occupied Ynys Môn and he prepared his forces to attack the mainland. Amongst his army were many Gascon knights and Spanish mercenaries. A bridge of boats was built across the Strait and the army started for the mainland led by the knights. On the opposite shore, the Welsh were well hidden and as the English army started to clamber ashore, they were suddenly attacked. Panic ensued and the English were unable to retreat as men were pouring over the bridge. The boats started swaying and many knights – in full armour – fell into the sea. Others were cut down by the Welsh arrows. Then the tide turned, and smashed the bridge of boats. About 30 knights, including their leader Luke de Tany, and over 200 soldiers perished on that day. Although the battle is known as The Battle of Moel-y-don, many historians believe that it took place further east; some say near Hirael in Bangor and some as far east as Abergwyngregyn.

Nelson's Statue: It was erected in 1873 as a navigational aid, in tribute to the famous admiral, by the Earl of Uxbridge of Plas Newydd.

Plas Coch: A stepped-gabled, three-storeyed 16th century house built of red sandstone on whose land there is now a caravan park. The Hughes family of Plas Coch was one of the famous families of the island in the 16th and early 17th centuries.

Plas Newydd: The home of the Marquesses of Anglesey and their forebears from the 16th century onwards. The precise date of the first house on the site is not known, but it was the second Baronet, Sir Nicholas Bayly (1707-1782) who made the first extensive alterations and the house began to look as it appears today. The most famous inhabitant was Henry Paget who lost a leg at the Battle of Waterloo. His exploits are chronicled in a military museum in the house. He was second in command in the battle and in recognition of his bravery he was created the first Marquess of Anglesey. The house which is now owned by the National Trust, contains a celebrated mural, painted between 1936 and 1940, by Rex Whistler.

Pont y Borth (The Menai Suspension Bridge) – was built in 1826 by Thomas Telford, the world's first large iron suspension bridge, spanning 579 feet and 100 feet above the water to allow high-masted sailing ships to pass underneath. The first 23 ton cable was lifted into place by a novel pulley system, involving 150 men kept in time by a fife band. They celebrated their achievement by running across the nine-inch-wide chain from the island to the mainland.

Porthaethwy (Menai Bridge): There was a community in the area at the time of the Welsh Princess (10th to 13th centuries) with scattered farms served by the Church of St Tysilio. There was a mill on the shore and numerous weirs to catch fish. But there were few roads apart from ones serving the ferries. During Victorian times, the town became a popular tourist destination with steam ships calling with day-trippers.

Pwll Ceris (The Swellies): A dangerous whirlpool in the Strait. In the 9th century it was described as one of the wonders of

Ynys Môn (Anglesey).

Pwllfanog: The quay is said to date back to the 16th century and was a small, flourishing harbour until about 1900, exporting slate for school writing tablets and milled flour. There was later a margarine factory and bacon factory here.

Y Felin Heli (Salt Mill): During the 16th century there was a mill here using the tidal waters to turn its wheel. There was also a fishing weir here.

Ynys Gorad Goch – contains the remains of a huge fish weir (gorad).

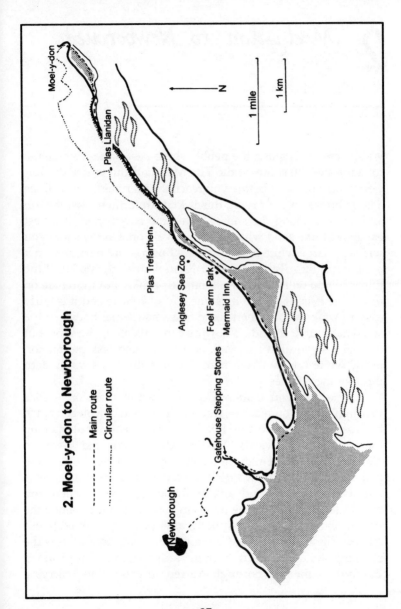

2. Moel-y-don to Newborough

- - - - - Main route
.... Circular route

Moel-y-don

Plas Llanidan

Plas Trefarthen

Anglesey Sea Zoo

Foel Farm Park

Mermaid Inn

Gatehouse Stepping Stones

Newborough

N

1 mile
1 km

27

2 Moel-y-don to Newborough

12 miles – 4 hours

Walk westwards along the pebbly shore past **Barras**, where the road reaches the shore, to the **The Mermaid Inn** where the **Tal-y-foel** ferry ran. Just before you reach the Mermaid, you will see a large house on your right, this is **Plas Trefarthen**. Past the Inn and proceed along the shore. If the tide is out there is a vast expanse of fine sand which you can walk on. On the shore you will see a large white house – **Plas y Borth** – and next door to it a modern house Tal-y-foel Stud Farm which offers B&B. If the tide is in you will have to walk on the pebbles, but from here on they have been flattened by some sort of vehicle and it is fairly easy to walk on. You then come to a small white house with a small harbour. If the tide is out you can walk along the shore but if otherwise you have to walk on private land (ask permission in the white house). From here onwards there is a sandy path through the pebbles.

Further on you come to a large white mansion – Plas Penrhyn. Then you reach a large sandbank which you can reach by crossing a small stream. It is tempting to walk straight along the sandbank towards **Trwyn Abermenai** and over to **Newborough Warren,** but the river Braint reaches the sea here and unless it is very low tide it is too deep to cross. If the tide is out, walk along the sandbank until you find a place where you can wade across. But if the tide is in you have to walk along the pebbly shore. You will eventually, after passing a ruined house on your right, arrive at the Gatehouse stepping stones. Cross the stepping stones, then turn back towards the sea and walk along the shore of the **Newborough Warren.** If you feel like carrying on walking, you can follow Route 3 to Malltraeth.

Otherwise, after crossing the stepping stones follow the track, past a farm, until you come to the main road. Turn left and follow the road to **Newborough.**

CIRCULAR ROUTE
11 miles – 3 ½ hours
This is the longest of the circular walks but half of it is along the beautiful Menai Strait and the rest across fields and along leafy lanes, with a break half-way at either the Anglesey Sea Zoo or Foel Farm Park. Therefore the 3½ hours only covers the walking!

Go along the A4080 from Llanfairpwll, past Plas Newydd and immediately after the wall ends you will see a sign for Moel-y-don. Follow this sign for a mile until you reach the shore and a small car park. Turn right and walk along the shore. You cannot do this walk at high tide because there are a couple of places where the water comes right up to private property. It is also much easier when the tide is out as there are sandy patches to walk on.

Along the shore past Castell Gwylan with Y Felinheli on the opposite side of the Strait, past a jetty with Plas Llanfair, the Plas Menai Water Sports Centre and the Friction Dynamics (scene of one of the longest recent strikes in Britain) on the other side of the water until you reach a road by a cottage. Onto this road and continue along the shore until you come to the Sea Zoo and Foel Farm Park (with its Chocolate Shop) further along.

Both these attractions are well worth a visit, if only for a sit down and some refreshments. The Sea Zoo is open all year round but the Farm Park only from March to October.

Back along the road and onto the shore. Look for a coastal footpath sign and over the stile into the field. Turn right and walk along the field aiming for a small gate with the impressive Plas Trefarthen on your left. Walk along the field nearer the house, not the one near the shore, aiming for a stile over a fence and another one immediately after it over a wall. Then straight across the field to a gate with a stone stile and a wooden post with yellow arrow.

Walk along the right hand side of the field along a wall to another gate and stone stile and then straight ahead along the track aiming for the woods. Turn left and over a stile and follow the path skirting the woods. The path then goes into the woods, eventually emerging by a stone stile. Walk diagonally across the field towards a gate and stone stile near Llanidan Farm, and then right, down a lane past **Plas Llanidan** with its peacocks on your right.

Then left up the lane through an avenue of trees and then right at the footpath sign and along a lane past Bryn Llwyd. At the junction, go straight ahead along the track rather than right. At the next junction, bear right and on past **Plas Porthamel** with its duck pond. Turn right here and go along the lane. At the junction, turn left. By Bron Menai follow the lane to the right until you come to a T-junction. Turn right and down the hill back to Moel-y-don.

PLACES OF INTEREST

Long Ship Inn: On the edge of Newborough Warren, close to the mouth of the Braint (near present day Pen-lôn) there used to be an ancient pub. The fishermen would moor their boats in the deepest part of the river, where it turns ninety degrees, and they would then walk towards Newborough calling at the Long Ship Inn on the way.

Mermaid Inn: It used to be called the Menai Hotel and people using the Tal-y-foel ferry used to stay there. At the time of writing the pub is closed.

Newborough, which was originally called Rhosyr, was settled about 1295 by the villagers of Llanfaes (hence new borough) who were evicted by Edward I when he built Beaumaris town and castle. The village became well known for its markets and fair, but with the clearing of trees high winds caused sand to engulf the farmland and during the time of Elizabeth I marram grass was planted to stabilise the sand dunes. The villagers used this grass until the 20th century to weave mats, ropes, baskets, fishing nets, brooms and filters for use in copper mines.

Newborough Warren: Cattle and sheep are grazed on the dunes. Despite the myxomatosis epidemic of 1954, many rabbits thrive in this favourable habitat. Together with Llanddwyn Beach, the warren forms a National Nature Reserve.

Plas Porthamel: A fortified camp used to be sited here. It is reputed that fallen Britons are buried nearby in Bryn y Beddau (Hill of the Graves).

Plas Trefarthen, the large white house, is on the possible site of a 1st century AD battle between the Britons and the Romans.

Plas Llanidan and Saint Nidan Church – dates back to the 15th century when it was radically altered. It was abandoned and partly demolished in 1844 when a new church was built near Brynsiencyn. The church has a unique stoup or small basin to hold holy water that is reputed to refill itself every time it is used. St Nidan is believed to have lived in the 7th century at Cadair Idan in the parish of Llanidan. He had connections with the large monastery of St Seiriol at Penmon. His holy well, Ffynnon Idan, is at Plas Llanidan about 200 yards from the old church. There was an Augustinian community here before the Dissolution of the Monasteries.

Tal-y-foel Ferry: The first passenger ferry from Tal-y-foel to Caernarfon sailed in 1425. In later years, passengers had to be carried ashore on the backs of the ferrymen as the shifting sands of Traeth Gwyllt made the crossing hazardous. The 'tallivoile' ferry was mentioned in accounts in 1503; pigs were transported in considerable numbers but people were advised not to cross here as the currents were treacherous. In 1849 a 75 foot long steamboat, the *Menai,* sailed between here and Caernarfon. Traeth Gwyllt remained a problem despite the building of a pier to accommodate boats at low water. The service ended on 30 July, 1954, when a bus service was started between Newborough and Caernarfon. The low jetty still stands on the beach.

Over the years a number of people using the ferry drowned. Seventy-nine people drowned in 1664 when it capsized, and another 30 people were lost in 1723.

Trwyn Abermenai: It is possibly here that the Romans first invaded Ynys Môn. First under Suetonis Paulinus in 60AD and later under Agricola in 78AD. Suetonius is said to have had a huge army of perhaps 10,000 soldiers, as well as cavalry. The soldiers are said to have been taken across in flat-bottomed boats brought from Chester, while the horses swam.

At one time a ferry crossed from here to the mainland by the people of Newborough taking their wares to Caernarfon but was not popular as no proper road was made to it. In 1725 Daniel Defoe used the Abermenai ferry on his way to Caergybi (Holyhead). In December 1785, the ferry boat hit the sandbank and was swamped by the rough seas near Caernarfon with the loss of 54 lives. Only one man survived – Huw Williams. There was another disaster to the east when the ferry from Barras capsized in 1820 and 22 people drowned. The only survivor was another Huw Williams!

3. Newborough to Malltraeth

- – – – – Main route
- .... Circular route

1 mile

1 km

N

Malltraeth

Cob Malltraeth

Traeth Malltraeth

Newborough

Newborough Forest

P

Ynys Llanddwyn

3 Newborough to Malltraeth

9 miles – 3 hours

Either continue your walk from Newborough Warren or walk from either Newborough through **Newborough Forest** or through Newborough Warren Nature Reserve. Alternatively you can park your car in the Newborough forest car park, which is only a few yards from the beach. Llanddwyn beach is a magnificent stretch of sand and an easy walk. Looking westwards you will see Ynys Llanddwyn, really a headland rather than an island but can be cut off at high tide. It is worth visiting the **lighthouse, pilot's cottages** and the remains of **St Dwynwen's church.**

Walk back from Llanddwyn Island and continue your walk in a north-westerly direction across the sand of Malltraeth Bay. Looking in a north-westerly direction you think that you can cross Malltraeth Sands but the river Cefni enters the sea here and you have to walk along its edge until you reach **Cob Malltraeth.** If you prefer a short cut, you can walk through some of the numerous tracks through Newborough Forest but you will miss the magnificent views across the sands.

Walk along Malltraeth Cob, cross the bridge over the river Cefni and into the village of **Malltraeth.** You may now return along the A4080 back to Newborough.

CIRCULAR ROUTE
between 4 and 12 miles and between 1½ and 3 hours
There is a choice of routes –
From Malltraeth to the beach and circular route   *3 hours*

34

From Malltraeth and circular route	1½ hours
From forest car park to beach	2½ hours
From forest car park – circular route	1½ hours

Either start from the car park at Malltraeth (opposite the Joiner's Arms and walk along Cob Malltraeth – well worth it as you can see herons fishing in the lakes) or from the car park in the woodland at the southern edge of Cob Malltraeth.

From the woodland car park follow the track on your right into the woods. You will then see a footpath to your right, follow this. The footpath runs parallel to a fence. There might be some wet patches here after heavy rain. After a while the path turns left and reaches a track. Turn right. Go past the first turning to your left. At the second turning*, you have a choice: either go straight ahead to the beach or turn left and follow the instructions given further on.

If you decide to go to the beach (it will add another hour to your journey), go straight ahead. You will eventually reach a junction with a grassy track going up to your right. Go straight ahead, the track now sweeps to the left. You will then see two large outcrops of rock to your left. You will also hear the sea by now. There is no path from here to the sea, but it is only a five minute walk through the woods to the beach.

Turn right into the woods and walk at 90° to the track, walking in the direction of where the sound of the sea comes from. You will have to come back this way, so try and remember which way you came. It might be an idea to leave a trail of sticks or stones so that you can find your way back easier. Through the forest until you come to a sandy track and a large dune in front of you. Cross the track and over the dune and you will arrive at Traeth Penrhos with Ynys Llanddwyn to your left.

Retrace your steps back to *, and turn right up the track. When you reach the edge of the forest, you will come to a junction, turn left. Carry on along the track, disregarding the tracks turning to your right. Go downhill to a T-junction, turn right along the track until you come to the main road. Here is a sign to the Wildlife Pool across the road. You might like to visit here; it will add another hour or so to your *journey.*

Otherwise, follow the footpath to your left which runs parallel to the road, back to the car park, and if you started from Malltraeth, back along Cob Malltraeth to the car park.

If you wish to visit Ynys Llanddwyn, go to Newborough and follow the sign to Llanddwyn. There is an admission charge to go down the forest road to the car park and toilets. You then walk along the beach to Ynys Llanddwyn where you can see the lighthouse, pilot's cottages with exhibition and the remains of St Dwynwen's church. Then back along the beach.

PLACE OF INTEREST

Cob Malltraeth – before the reclamation of the land, the estuary of the Cefni stretched almost to the A5 and boats reached as far as Llangefni where there was a small quay. Early in the 19th century, the Cob or embankment was built in order to gain farmland from the sea with the river Cefni being turned into a canal. A road was built along the cob to enable farmers to take their produce to the Menai ferries to be sold in Caernarfon market. Behind the cob is a lagoon called Pwll Malltraeth which is home to numerous birds. Charles Tunnicliffe, the famous wildlife artist, spent the last 30 years of his life here making drawings of the birds he could see from his studio which overlooks the estuary.

Cors Malltraeth or Cors Ddyga: Coal mining took place here for many centuries and barges carried the coal from Malltraeth, much of it to provide fuel for copper smelting at Amlwch on the eastern side of the island.

Lighthouse, lifeboat and pilot's cottages at Llanddwyn: Pilot's Cove, at the extreme tip of the island, was formed in the early 19th century when a causeway was built to connect it to a small island. Cottages were built for salvagemen who would go out to help stricken ships. Since the area was dangerous to shipping due to the shifting sandbanks, a lifeboat was established in 1840.

In 1861, the lifeboat house – which still remains – was built. A new boat was delivered in 1885 but the service ended in 1907. Later on, Llanddwyn became a pilot station where a pilot was taken aboard by vessels heading up the channel to Caernarfon or Y Felinheli – both busy slate exporting ports.

At the beginning of the 19th century, a white stone tower was erected close to Pilot's Cove to aid shipping but it was not a success and a larger stone tower was built in 1846. It had a red oil lamp that was illuminated at night. From 1972 the light has been automatic.

Four pilots and two apprentices were drowned in January 1874 while attempting to take a pilot off the schooner *Margaret* in strong wind. The capsized pilot boat came ashore in Dinas Dinlle near Caernarfon.

Malltraeth – means 'rotting dene' or salt marsh. At one time, Viking longships and traders sailed up the river through the marsh (Cors Ddyga). Ships were built and repaired here at the end of the 18th century.

Newborough Forest: Fifty years ago it was just sand-dunes. Today it produces some 10,000 tons of timber annually. Neolithic man lived here and relics from his past have been discovered, including mounds of shells.

On the edge of the forest are the foundations of a medieval court which was one of several small courts on Ynys Môn where the Princes of Aberffraw would have stayed while travelling the island to collect rents and to hold courts of law. Centuries of sand covered the base of the hall and other buildings. Masonry is several courses high and the items found includes 13th and 14th century pottery.

Near the car park by the beach (to the right when you are entering it) are the remains of an old cottage which had been buried in the sands for centuries. It is probably one of the houses of Rhosyr, which according to tradition, is buried under the sands. In the 14th century huge storms blew sand inland overwhelming eleven cottages.

St Dwynwen's church: St Dwynwen came here in the 5th century after a failed love affair with Prince Maelon and devoted her life to God. She became the patron saint of Welsh lovers and a church was established here in the late 15th, early 16th century. Today little remains of the church; it is said, that about two hundred years ago, the timber was removed by local people to build ships.

Nearby used to be St Dwynwen's well where its miraculous waters (with the help of a sacred eel) allowed hopeful lovers to ascertain the depth of their partner's faithfulness towards them. A cross was erected close to the lighthouse to Saint Dwynwen in 1897.

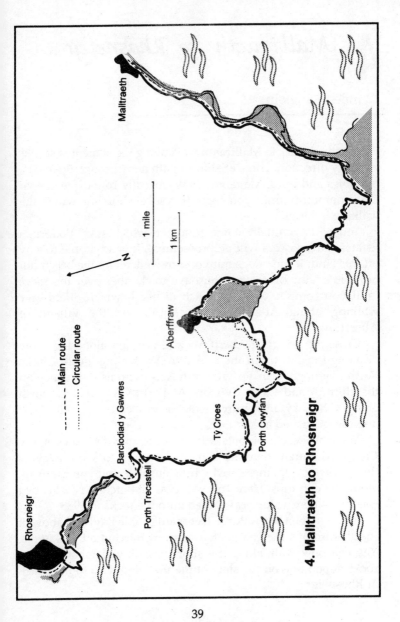

Rhosneigr

Barclodiad y Gawres

Porth Trecastell

Tŷ Croes

Porth Cwyfan

Aberffraw

Malltraeth

- - - - Main route
.... Circular route

N

1 mile
1 km

4. Malltraeth to Rhosneigr

4 Malltraeth to Rhosneigr

12 miles – 4½ hours

From the car park in Malltraeth walk along the shore in a south-westerly direction. There are bits of path here through the reeds, brambles and mud. Make you way carefully round the **Trwyn Du** promontory until you come to a level shoreline where the walking is easier.

You will eventually come to a sign which says 'Bodorgan Estates – trespassers will be prosecuted'. It is advisable to stay off this land. If the tide is out you can walk along the beach out of harm's way; otherwise you have to clamber over the rocks until you come to a wide stretch of beach which offers easy walking along Aberffraw Sands towards the village of **Aberffraw**.

Cross the bridge at Aberffraw and turn left along the shore or along the cliff top if the tide is in. Walk along Porth China, Porth Lleidiog, Porth Terfyn, Porth Aels (with its iron winch on the clifftop) and Porth Cwyfan. At Porth Cwyfan it is worth going to **St Cwyfan's church** which is located on a small island and can be visited at low tide.

You now reach the outskirts of the former **Tŷ Croes Army Camp**. Although there are signs telling you to keep away as there is live firing, these are by now obsolete and you can walk along the cliff tops. Here you will pass a stretch of coast called Caethle, where a ship was driven onto the rocks in 1938.

You will then reach **Porth Trecastell** (Cable Bay) and above it (northwards) is the chambered cairn of **Barclodiad y Gawres**. You can now walk along the shore, possibly clambering over rocks depending on the state of the tide, and onto to the beach at **Rhosneigr**.

CIRCULAR ROUTE

2½ miles – 1 hour

Park your car by the old bridge in Aberffraw. On the village side, walk along the lane that runs along the river Ffraw. At the end of the lane, follow the path between the wall and the river or if the tide is out you can walk along the sand.

Go past the white bungalow on your right and go past the track running inland after it. Go through the kissing gate on your right, up the path to a junction near Trwyn Du, bear left. At the next junction, bear left again and straight ahead towards the sea until you reach the beach at Porth Aels.

Then follow the footpath to your right that takes you inland. Before taking this path, you will notice that there is a path that follows the coast; you can follow this if you want and then retrace your steps to this point. Along the path inland and then left to kissing gate and onto track.

Up the track and then right along another track. Go past a white farmhouse on your left, and straight ahead through a kissing gate onto a path. Through a series of kissing gates until you reach some houses and go down the road to a T-junction. Turn left by the school and go past **St Beuno's Church** on your left before turning right past the village hall on your right and down hill to the village square.

Go straight across, past Y Goron pub and down to where you parked your car.

PLACES OF INTEREST

Aberffraw: In the Welsh bardic tradition it is one of the three pre-eminent tribal thrones of Britain. It was probably the seat of Maelgwn, King of Gwynedd, as early as the mid 6th century. Later, between the 9th and 13th centuries, it was the principal court of the Welsh princes until Llywelyn ein Llyw Olaf (The Last) was killed in 1282. The remains of the palace probably lie below the Maes Llywelyn housing estate. In 1317, 198 eight lengths of timber were removed from the hall and other buildings and used to build Caernarfon castle. Nevertheless, as late as the 18th century it was still possible to trace the last vestiges of the palace in the south-west corner of the village. After a number of Viking raids from Ireland in the 13th century, the main base for the Princes became Abergwyngregyn on the mainland. The Llys Llywelyn heritage centre, telling the story of the Princes and the whole of Ynys Môn, is situated in a building nearby.

The bridge at Aberffraw was built in 1731 by Sir A Owen of Bodowen, an estate to the east of the village. In the 18th century it had a significant shipbuilding industry until the estuary silted up. According to the Welsh heroic tales y Mabinogi, the wedding feast of Branwen and Matholwch, king of Ireland, was held at Aberffraw.

Stealing from wrecks was common along this coast during the 18th and 19th centuries. In 1823 the *Flora* was lost with all hands off Aberffraw. Later, two men were found guilty of stealing some its cargo and not only were they imprisoned for six months but, on their release, they were publicly flogged at Aberffraw before a large crowd.

Barclodiad y Gawres: This is a cruciform passage grave, comprising a long narrow passage leading to a central chamber with three side chambers. Some of the stones are decorated with abstract designs including spirals, zigzags a lozenges. Cremated bones were found inside it. It was originally covered by a mound but it has now a concrete and glass dome to protect it through which you can see the stones. You can walk into the passage up to an iron gate but if you want to go further you will have to obtain keys from The Wayside Shop in Llanfaelog.

Caethle: In 1938 the streamer *Kyle Prince* was carrying cement from Barry in south Wales to Liverpool when she ran into trouble near Ynys Enlli (Bardsey Island) off the Llŷn peninsula. Water flooded into the ship, dowsing the fires and the gales blew her towards Anglesey. The Holyhead lifeboat eventually reached her and took off the crew. Cables were used to secure the ship, but they broke and she was driven onto the rocks at Caethle and smashed to bits.

This was the site of the first attempt, in the 1850s, to lay an electric telegraph cable to Ireland. All attempts failed, but it was eventually successful further south at Porth Trecastell.

Porth Trecastell (Cable Bay) – was the eastern terminus of the undersea electric telegraph cable to Ireland which then linked it with the transatlantic cable.

Rhosneigr: In the 1800s, Rhosneigr consisted of a coastguard station and a dozen or so houses belonging to fishermen who made their living mainly by catching lobsters. In 1863 the Maelog Hotel was built among the dunes by Evan Thomas of Liverpool, a member of the famous family of bonesetters from Anglesey. There was considerable opposition to this development, both by the local farmers who feared for their grazing rights and also by the local temperance society! Guards were posted to guard the site, but in October 1863 one of these guards was thrown into a lake and the partially built hotel blown up. Seventeen men were jailed. The hotel was eventually completed, proving to be a great attraction to the newly developing tourist trade. Soon Rhosneigr became a bustling holiday resort.

In 1930 the airship R101 was seen over the village as the mother of one of the pilots lived in Rhosneigr.

There was a lifeboat here between 1872 and 1924. It cost £680 to build the station – money donated by the widow of a man drowned nearby. The lifeboat over the years saved 73 lives.

Saint Beuno's church contains a fine example of a 12th century Romanesque arch. The south door is 14th century and the north aisle added in the 16th century. A Norman arch which may be the only surviving part of the Prince's palace is part of the church.

Saint Cwyfan's church: It is a simple church on a small island linked to the mainland by a causeway. Cwyfan was probably a monk and disciple of Saint Beuno, whom he accompanied to

43

north Wales in the 7th century. He is thought to be Irish. The single cell church may be 12th century with a north aisle added in the 16th century. The surrounding wall was built in the 19th century to protect the island from the sea. Occasional services are held here during the summer.

Trwyn Du: Here, 9,000 years ago, were temporary communities of hunting a food-gathering people. Scatterings of flint flakes and other waste material from the making of harpoons and arrows have been found here. The low grass mound is all that remains of a much later monument – an Early Bronze Age (1700BC) cairn sealed by stones.

Tŷ Croes Army Camp: A former army camp, now used for motorcycle racing. The name originally derived from a house 'with a wing attached' and was later used for the settlement that grew here after the opening of the railway station in 1848.

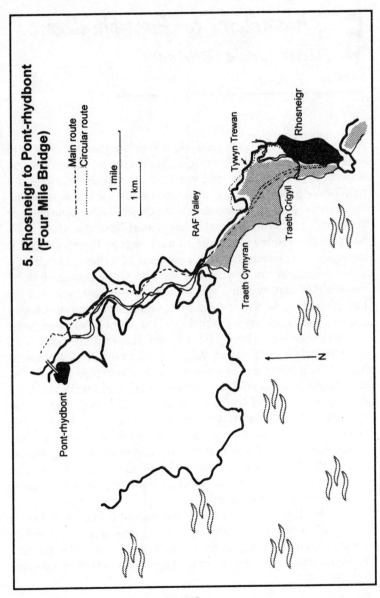

5. Rhosneigr to Pont-rhydbont (Four Mile Bridge)

Main route
Circular route

1 mile
1 km

Pont-rhydbont

RAF Valley

Tywyn Trewan

Rhosneigr

Traeth Cymyran

Traeth Crigyll

N

45

5 Rhosneigr to Pont-rhydbont (Four Mile Bridge)

7 miles – 3½ hours

At Rhosneigr, walk on to the beach (there are plenty of places to park in the village) and bear right. At the edge of the village you will come to a small stream; you can either walk inland about half a mile to a footbridge, walk back along the beach to where the stream reaches the sea and is much shallower or take your boots off and walk through the water! You can then walk barefoot for about half a mile as the beach at **Traeth Crigyll** is very sandy. Towards **Traeth Cymyran** it becomes more pebbly. After about two miles you will see two white houses; behind these is **RAF Valley** and if you walk up to the dunes you will see the hangars (you will, probably, have already seen and heard the jets and helicopters practising). Turn right before you come to the houses and follow a track by the side of RAF Valley.

If the tide is out you can walk along the sandy beach towards Ynys Las. If not, there is a bit of a scramble before you! By the RAF landing lights go down to the shoreline and walk along the edge. In some places you will have to scramble over rocks. After rounding the headland you will come to a marshy headland; walk along the edge (do not venture across it as it is very muddy in places). You will see that the estuary extends a distance to your right, but you do not have to walk to its far end. Look for stepping stones that cross a stream; cross these and you come to a track, follow it to your left.

The track then turns inland, but do not follow it. Follow a faint path around the shore until you come to a line of stones (embankment) crossing the bay. There is a path on this embankment. Left after the embankment and clamber up some

46

rocks and walk along the edge of a field until you come to some steps which takes you down to the shore. If the tide is in you will have to clamber over some more rocks.

By a small caravan park (there were four caravans when I was there last) you come to a track which you follow, but not as it turns inland. You will have to go up some more rocks, and then walk as far as possible along the cliff top alongside a fence until it is possible to make your way down to the beach. Follow the faint path to a small bay and walk around its edge to a small embankment near a farmhouse.

Cross this embankment and continue along the shoreline until you come to a low embankment. Walk across it, then over a stile and then follow the path until you come to a lane near a farm. You will then reach the B4545, turn left and cross the bridge to **Pont-rhydbont.**

CIRCULAR ROUTE
5 miles – 2 hours
Park at the free car park in Rhosneigr near the library and toilets. Walk down the hill to the junction and turn right. Walk along the main street until you reach the war memorial and clock. Turn left down the hill and onto the beach. Turn right and walk along the beach until you come to a river. Walk alongside the river until it becomes shallow enough to cross. You will have to take your boots and socks off, but then you can walk barefoot along the sands of Traeth Crigyll. If you don't want to get your feet wet, walk inland alongside the river until you come to a wooden footbridge, cross it and then walk back along onto the beach.

*Walk as far as the end of the beach and then around the headland. Look for a path that takes you up into the dunes. You will now see RAF Valley ahead of you and possibly planes taking off and landing. You will have heard the planes practising when you reached Rhosneigr. Look for a path that runs alongside a small fence which has red and white poles every tenth pole. Follow this path onto **Tywyn Trewan.***

After you have passed a high fence and some sheds on the RAF land, the fence turns right. Look for a path following the fence. Then the fence goes left, but follow the path straight ahead aiming for a wooden footbridge.

Over the bridge and follow the track towards the houses, then up a lane between the houses. Then, by a large square building, turn left and walk to the main road. Turn right and walk back into the village and into the car park.

PLACES OF INTEREST

Pont-rhydbont (Four Mile Bridge): The old post road to Caergybi crosses a bridge (pont) here – where the sea is narrowest – to Ynys Cybi. Before building the Stanley Embankment, this was the only road to Caergybi. The bridge was built in 1675, but it is believed that there was a bridge here before then, and even before then, as its Welsh name suggests, a ford (rhyd). A milestone was placed here in 1752, and as it was the fourth from Caergybi it got its English name, Four Mile Bridge.

RAF Valley – was established in 1941 and was used from 1943 to 1945 as the United States Air Force Transatlantic Terminal for flights to Britain. It is now used to train fighter pilots. It is also the base for 22 Squadron Air-Sea Rescue whose yellow helicopters have saved countless lives in the Snowdonia mountains and along the north Wales coast.

During the winter of 1942/3, peat was extracted from the edges of Llyn Cerrig Bach to consolidate the sand dunes on which the runways were built, as wind blown sand from the dunes was damaging the planes' engines. When the local men started moving the peat they began to discover iron and bronze objects mixed with animal bones. They turned out to represent one of the most important collections of Iron Age material in the British Isles and can now be seen in the National Museum of Wales in Cardiff. They include spears, daggers, plaques, bridle-

Y Felinheli on the opposite side of the Strait taken from Moel-y-don.

Britannia Bridge – the gateway to Ynys Môn (Anglesey).

Remains of Tal-y-foel Ferry pier with the Eryri (Snowdonia) mountains in the background.

Gatehouse Stepping Stones crossing afon Braint at low tide.

St Dwynwen's Cross

Llanddwyn lighthouse

Ynys Llanddwyn – a popular destination for all lovers.

Porth Trecastell (Cable Bay) *from where
an undersea electric telegraph cable ran to Ireland.*

The old bridge at Aberffraw was built in 1731.

Rhosneigr a popular tourist destination.

*Traeth Crigyll – where the infamous Lladron Crigyll
lured ships on to rocks.*

Trearddur Bay – a magnet for visitors.

*St Gwenfaen's Well – one of the best preserved holy wells
on Anglesey.*

South Stack lighthouse on Ynys Lawd.

Tŵr Elin – an RSPB observatory where you can see hundreds of nesting birds.

Holyhead Breakwater – 1.5 miles long, built at a cost of £1,285,000 between 1845 and 1873.

A high speed ferry leaving Holyhead for Ireland.

Gorad Alaw – an old fish weir near Valley.

Ynysoedd y Moelrhoniaid (The Skerries) *– graveyard to many ships.*

Bwthyn Swtan — the last thatched cottage on Ynys Môn (Anglesey).

CODWYD Y GOFEB HON
I DDATHLU
CAN MLWYDD A HANNER
SEFYDLU A LANSIO'R
BAD–ACHUB CYNTAF AR
YNYS MÔN
1828 – 1978
SEFYDLWYD GAN Y PARCH. JAMES WILLIAMS
A FRANCES WILLIAMS
ERECTED TO COMMEMORATE
THE ONE HUNDRED AND FIFTIETH
ANNIVERSARY OF ESTABLISHING
AND LAUNCHING THE FIRST
LIFE BOAT
ON THE ISLE OF ANGLESEY
1828 – 1978
ESTABLISHED BY THE REV. JAMES WILLIAMS
AND FRANCES WILLIAMS

Monument near Cemaes commemorating the establishing of the first lifeboat on Ynys Môn.

Cemaes harbour – once an important port and ship building centre, now home to pleasure boats.

The former brickworks at Porth Llanlleinana.

The old brick kilns at Porth Wen.

Porth Amlwch – from where thousands of tons of copper ore was exported in the 18th and 19th century.

The large mansion Portobello on Traeth Dulas.

Point Lynas Lighthouse, has a static light rather than a revolving one.

*The Royal Charter Monument, commemorating the death
of over 400 people.*

Ynys Seiriol (Puffin Island), *where at one time puffins were caught, pickled and sent to English cities.*

Penmon monastery built in the 12th century with the 16th century dovecote on the right.

Victoria Terrace, Beaumaris, designed by Joseph Hansom of Hansom cab fame.

Beaumaris pier and beach with the magnificent Eryri (Snowdonia) mountains in the background.

bits, chains, harnesses, shield bosses and decorative bronze-work.

Traeth Crigyll: This beach was once well known for Lladron Crigyll (The Wreckers of Crigyll) who lured ships onto the shore so that they could steal their cargoes. In 1715 three men were sent to Beaumaris Gaol after being found guilty of raiding the sloop *The Charming Jenny* that was stranded in the river Crigyll (which at one time went one mile inland). On another occasion in December 1740 the Liverpool brigantine *Loveday and Betty* came ashore in a gale and the captain went for assistance. On his return, he found the vessel stripped of everything, including the sails. Three local men appeared before Beaumaris Assizes. Everyone expected them to be hanged but the judge was so drunk that he discharged them! On 30 November 1867, *The Times* reported that "The Wreck *(Earl of Chester)* is now prey to the notorious wreckers of the coast known ... as Lladron Grigyll. Many hundreds of them were there yesterday stealing whatever they could carry away."

In 1876 ten men were saved from the *Clifton* by the Rhosneigr lifeboat after it had foundered on the Crigyll reef. Two years later, a Dutch brigantine, the *Elizabeth Klousterboer* came to grief on the same rocks. The lifeboat was able to find only one survivor.

Traeth Cymyran: The wreck of the clipper *Norman Court* lies off Traeth Cymyran. In March 1883, she was carrying sugar from Java when she hit rocks. Her mast collapsed and with the sea breaking over her, the crew clung to the fore-rigging. The Rhoscolyn lifeboat was not available, so the crew had to use a rowing boat. They were rowing against the wind and it was impossible to get to the ship. A message was sent to the Holyhead lifeboat crew who came by a special train and were able to launch a lifeboat which got to the ship and saved the lives of the crew. The coxswain received the RNLI silver medal for his bravery.

Tywyn Trewan: At the beginning of the last century there were plans to build an ammunition factory here providing jobs for over 300 people, but the hoteliers and visitors to Rhosneigr opposed the development and it was never built.

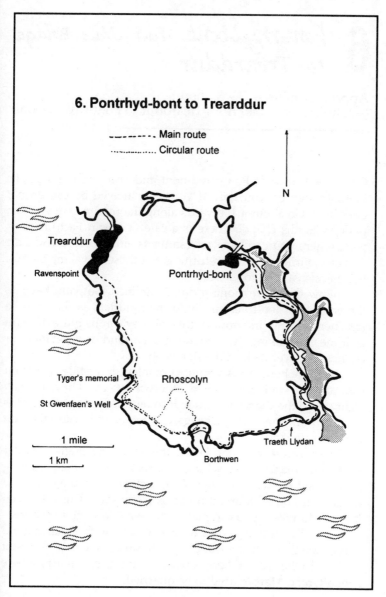

6. Pontrhyd-bont to Trearddur

- – – – – – Main route
- .... Circular route

N

Trearddur

Ravenspoint

Pontrhyd-bont

Tyger's memorial

Rhoscolyn

St Gwenfaen's Well

1 mile

1 km

Traeth Llydan

Borthwen

6 Pont-rhyd-bont (Four Mile Bridge) to Trearddur

Approx 10 miles – 3 – 3½ hours
(+ ½ hour along road from Trearddur to Pont-rhyd-y-bont)

Cross the bridge at Pont-rhyd-bont and you will see a public footpath sign on your left. If you have arrived by car, do not park here. Go about a 100 yards along the road where you can park by Sardis chapel. There is a cafe (Y Gegin Fach) here as well, where you can have refreshments either before you start on your journey or when returning. For those travelling by bus, there is also a bus stop here.

Follow the shore along a poorly defined footpath. Keep to the edge and don't venture onto the mudflats as they can be treacherous. The first hour of this journey can be quite difficult as it means walking through ankle-deep mud or vegetation, or clambering over rocks if the tide is out.

The shore here forms a number of inlets. If the tide is out you can carefully walk across them; otherwise you will have to walk right round the shoreline. You will come across one or two paths leading from the shore. Disregard these as they can take you onto private land.

Before you reach Craig Dinas, there is a long finger of water stretching inland and reaching to a rock. Rather than walking right round the water's edge you can clamber up the rock via a rough path, on all-fours, through gorse bushes. This takes you into a field where you can make your way down to the shore.

You will eventually come to another inlet with a wall and old sluice gate that you can walk across to save some time and boot leather. To the west of here is Bodior with its old quarry where **Mona Green Marble** used to be quarried.

To your left you will see the hangars of RAF Valley and the sand on which you walked on the previous journey. With the tide in, you will have to clamber over the rocks or even venture into the vegetation (if you are walking in shorts, it is advisable to take a pair of strong trousers with you for these occasions); otherwise you can walk on golden sandbanks. The difficult part is now over and it is fairly easy from here onwards.

If you are walking on the cliff edge, you will come to a little fisherman's hut. There are steps here to take you down to the shore, where you can cross to another inlet.

You will now see the open sea and, if the wind is from the right direction, waves crashing on the rocks. Walking along the cliff top you will come to a castellated building; possibly a summer house at one time.

Below is the beach of Traeth Llydan (Silver Bay) for you to walk on. Out at sea there is the Rhoscolyn beacon on Ynys y Gwylanod. Then back onto the cliffs, with a pine forest to your right, walk until you come to the beach at Borthwen with the Old **Lifeboat** house. Disregard the roads running off the beach and carry on along the cliff top where there is a fairly well marked path, with styles and footbridges, which takes you past **St Gwenfaen's Well,** around **Rhoscolyn Head**. Out to sea you will see a solitary rock; this is Maen Piscar. On the side of the path here is a stone memorial to **Tyger** the dog.

Carry on along the clifftop until you come to a caravan site with a kissing gate into the site. There are three ways which you can now use. Either keep along the shore across a small bay and clamber up the cliffs; then follow the cliff until you rejoin the path. You can go through the kissing gate, and either turn left and walk along one of the lanes through the camp, or turn right along one of the lanes – both will bring you back to the path.

Proceed until you come to a small beach with a path turning right between two parallel stone walls. You cannot go further along the coast as you will reach a deep gully which you can't cross (unless you're a rock climber and the tide is out) as it reaches right up to private gardens. Follow the path until you reach a road. Turn left along the road and carry on until you reach Ravenspoint housing estate on your left. You can now follow a path that goes over rocky outcrops, past Porth Castell and Porth Diana, and on to the beach at Trearddur.

You can now either stay in **Trearddur** ready for the next stage, or walk (or even take a bus) back along the B4545 to Pont-rhyd-bont.

As I mentioned, the first hour is the difficult part. Therefore an alternative route would be to turn south off the main road by Sardis Chapel and follow the road through the village towards Rhoscolyn. You will pass the camping site at Pentre Iago and the road to Traeth Llydan (Silver Bay) on your left. The road then forks; take the left and follow the road past The White Eagle Inn. Follow it for another 800 yards and after a sharp left hand bend, turn right over a stile and follow the footpath past some houses and onto the northern side of Borthwen beach. You can now follow the coastal path to Trearddur as for the first route above.

CIRCULAR ROUTE
4 miles – $1\frac{1}{2}$ hours

From the village of Rhoscolyn drive past the Church of St Gwenfaen, taking the road to your left and then a narrow lane to your right, signposted To the Beach. Follow this lane till you come to a car park with toilets near Borthwen beach. This car park can be very full in summer; you may be able to park by the church and start this walk from there.

Walk onto Borthwen beach, then right towards steps by a concrete wall. Walk along this footpath, then down to a beach and back up along a track. Bear right by the Old Lifeboat house, walking up to a white house where you will see yellow arrows on the wall to your right by a house called Yr Allt.

Walk along the footpath past a coastguard lookout, with another lookout to your right, until you reach St Gwenfaen's Well. Follow the path alongside a stone wall until you come to Porth Saint. From here you can either return or go on ahead to see the memorial to Tyger the dog. This will take an extra half hour. Go past the next cove and before you reach a large white house you will see five stones to the left of the footpath. Tyger's memorial is the first one. Then return to Porth Saint.

Go over the stile on your right (on your left if you've visited Tyger's memorial), across the field to another stile which takes you onto an ancient trackway. Follow the yellow signs around the white farmhouse to a kissing gate and sign and go left along the lane until you reach the Church of St Gwenfaen. Take the road to the right and then the lane to the beach past the White Eagle Inn and back to the car park where you started.

PLACES OF INTEREST

Church of Saint Gwenfaen: The church was established here in the 6th century. It was rebuilt between 1871 and 1879 but baptisms are still conducted at the 15th century font saved from the old church.

Mona Green Marble: The stone was discovered at the end of the 18th century and was highly prized. One of the most prestigious pieces made from this marble was a magnificent table which was sent to Elba to be part of the furnishings of a large bungalow built for Napoleon Bonaparte.

Rhoscolyn: In the 19th century the waters off Rhoscolyn were famous for its oyster beds. Small, strongly built boats were used to dredge the oysters that lay a few miles offshore. They were brought ashore and laid upon the beach below the high water mark to mature in size before being loaded onto sloops to be taken to Liverpool.

Rhoscolyn Head: The *Southern Cross* sank off here in 1855 after striking a submerged rock in thick fog. Although the crew of 17 managed to escape in the ship's lifeboat, they struck another rock before reaching shore. They managed to scramble onto a large rock but were stranded for 12 hours before they were rescued by Rhoscolyn lifeboat.

Rhoscolyn Lifeboat: Established in 1831, between 1866 and 1881 Rhoscolyn lifeboat saved 102 lives. A memorial at Rhoscolyn church commemorates the crews. Yn 1901, while assisting the crew of the *JW Wearing* near Porth Saint, the lifeboat and the schooner collided, smashing four of the lifeboat's oars. Another oar was driven into its side. One of the crew, George Smith, severed it with an axe to get them away. Some years later, when he was over 80, Smith was himself rescued by the lifeboat after spending 18 hours clinging to the Rhoscolyn Beacon. He had been visiting his lobster pots when his boat smashed against a rock in a sudden gale.

In 1920, five members of the crew – including the coxswain – lost their lives trying to save the crew of the steamship *Timbo* in 80mph winds. As the *Timbo* was holding her anchors, the lifeboat turned back and made for the shelter of Llanddwyn. It took seven hours to get there and it was during this time that the five were swept overboard. The crew of the *Timbo* eventually launched their own lifeboat but four members lost their lives. The steamship broke her anchors and was blown onto the beach at Dinas Dinlle near Caernarfon. The lifeboat station closed in 1929 but the lifeboat house is still to be seen at Borthwen.

Saint Gwenfaen's Well: This is one of the best preserved holy wells on the island and was a place of pilgrimage for centuries. It consists of two sunken rooms and an enclosed pool. The well was associated with curing mental disorders by throwing two white quartz pebbles into the water. If bubbles arose there would be a miracle.

Towyn Lodge: A Georgian house which was occupied for a period by Thomas Telford while the London to Holyhead road (the present day A5) was built. It is said that he used the small tower in a corner of the garden overlooking Porth Diana as his workroom.

Trearddur: The old name for Trearddur was Tywyn y Capel but the name of a nearby farm called Tre Arddur (or Tre Iarddur) was adopted to distinguish it from another Tywyn y Capel. Iarddur was descended from Rhodri Fawr.

Tyger: Opposite Maen Piscar (which is about three-quarters of a mile from the shore) is a two foot high stone memorial to 'Tyger, September 17, 1819' which commemorates the devotion of a dog who helped to save the lives of four people following a shipwreck. A Liverpool-bound ketch struck Maen Piscar on a foggy night. As it sank Tyger, the captain's retriever, jumped into the sea and started to swim. His master, two sailors and a boy followed him. The boy clung onto Tyger's collar and he was dragged ashore. The dog then went back and seized one of the sailors by his collar and dragged him ashore. They were all exhausted but recovered – apart from Tyger who licked his master's hand and then died from exhaustion.

Tywyn y Capel Mound: About twenty yards above high water mark behind the seafront at Trearddur are the remains of an Early Christian chapel surrounded by a cemetery. The chapel, dedicated to Saint Bridget (the patron saint of the present church) was still standing in 1780 but the site has suffered from erosion over the years. Recent excavations have uncovered a number of burials, some set in stone-lined long 'cists' while later ones (mid 7th century) above were simple dug graves and included the remains of children. Bridget is believed to arrived on Ynys Môn from Ireland floating on a sod.

7. Trearddur to Caergybi (Holyhead)

- - - - - Main route
.... Circular route

1 mile

1 km

North Stack

Breakwater

Soldier's Point

P

South Stack
Lighthouse

Caer y Twr

Elin's Tower

Caergybi

N

Porth Ruffydd   Porth Dafarch

Trearddur

7 Trearddur to Caergybi (Holyhead)

9 miles – 5½ hours

If arriving by car, by garage turn down Lôn Isallt towards the Trearddur Bay Hotel where there is a large car park. Cross the road and onto the shore. You can either walk on the rocky shore or on the pavement. On your left there is a footpath running alongside a wall (with a large chalet in a field behind the wall). Walk along the pebbly beach until you see a large spooky-looking house built on the rock. The author **Nicholas Monserrat** *(The Cruel Sea)* is reputed to have lived here at one time.

Up the lane to your left, past the spooky house, then turn off the lane to a footpath to your left and follow the footpath over some rocks reaching a bungalow and white house. You will then come back to the road. Either walk on the beach or on the pavement until you come to a footpath on your left, marked Anglesey Coastal Path; follow it until you again reach the road by a large white house with red-tiled roof.

Again follow a footpath to your left until you reach a white bungalow. Go over a stile (broken when I last went over it), turn left down a lane and then onto the footpath which you follow until you reach the road again at **Porth Dafarch.** Near the path is a plaque to commemorate the author of the hymn *Rock of Ages.* Inland from here are the remains of a Neolithic settlement known locally as **Cytiau'r Gwyddelod**.

Take the footpath to your left which takes you along the cliff with magnificent views. There are numerous footpaths to follow here. Either take the one nearest the cliff edge or the shortest!

One of the coves that you will reach is **Porth Ruffydd** with steps running down to it. This used to a lifeboat station and you will see a small plaque commemorating this.

When you have walked about 1½ hours from Trearddur, you will see the **South Stack lighthouse** in the distance. You will eventually reach a farm track running inland. You are strongly advised to follow this as agricultural land reaches to the cliff edge at Porth y Gwyddel. Trying to walk between the fence and the cliff edge is *extremely dangerous*. Otherwise you can ask at the nearest farmhouse to walk across their land.

Walk up the track to a parking area at Gors Goch. This is the boring bit as you have to turn left onto a road. Within about a mile you will reach a junction, bear left and up a hill passing a pillar with 'Trinity House, London, 1809' on it.

If you miss seeing the sea for a while, after the road junction but before you reach Henborth farm, you will see a footpath to your left which takes you to a small cove and a footpath running for a few yards along the cliff. You cannot walk further along the coast, and you will have to go back onto the road and carry on up the hill until, after passing Plas Nico, you see a sign on your right to **Cytiau Gwyddelod Tŷ Mawr** and left to **Elin's Tower**.

You can make a detour and visit this Iron Age settlement but as the object is to walk the coast of Anglesey return to this spot and turn left along a footpath to the cliff edge with magnificent cliff views, and at the right time of the year, teeming with birds. You will then reach RSPB's Elin's Tower with its bird observatory.

Follow the path up the cliff in the direction of **South Stack lighthouse** on Ynys Lawd. If you feel energetic you can go down the steps, over a bridge and into the lighthouse. Otherwise, back onto the road until you reach the entrance to the path that leads you down to the lighthouse. Up the path until you reach an old Second World War observation post. There are a number of paths to follow, most over the top of **Mynydd Caergybi** *(Holyhead Mountain)* with one following the cliff edge to **Ynys Arw** *(North Stack)* and Parliament Cave, so called because of the cacophony of sound from the birds nesting in it.

If you go over the mountain you will reach a radio station with its large aerials and dishes. On the summit is the prehistoric hill fort of **Caer y Tŵr**. Once you have gone over the mountain, you will have a magnificent view of **Caergybi (Holyhead)** and its S-shaped **Breakwater** snaking out to sea, with the Irish ferries making their way in and out of the harbour.

Walking down the path you will see on your left a monument to some American airmen who were killed when their B24 crashed into Mynydd Caergybi in 1944. You will then reach **Breakwater Park**. You can either follow the path to you left or visit the Park where there are toilets and refreshments and wander around the old buildings.

Otherwise make your way to the shore and follow the path eastwards. You will pass on your right a solid-looking white building; this is the magazine where explosives were kept during the building of the Breakwater. Carry on along the path until you come to the Breakwater.

Here you will see a castelled building. This is Soldiers' Point which once guarded the entrance to **Caergybi (Holyhead)**. It is extremely difficult to follow the shore here, so my advice is to go around Soldiers' Point along a small lane, passing some imposing but derelict large house (a former hotel) until you again reach the shore by a sign warning you not to dive near the wreck of the *SS Castilian* which sank with explosives onboard.

Walk along the promenade past the **Lifeboat** House until you reach the old Lifeboat House which is now a maritime museum. Up the steps, along Beach Road and down to the **Harbour**, where the ferries sail to Ireland, by the Marine Hotel. Here, turn right along the road which takes you alongside the railway line past **Saint Cybi's Church** eventually reaching the main road which crosses the railway.

You have reached the end of the walk. Either stay in Caergybi's numerous hotels and B&Bs or make your way back to Trearddur along the B4545. The walk will take about half an hour or there is a regular bus service.

CIRCULAR ROUTE
5 miles – 1½ hours
This is the most mountainous and most strenuous circular route but well worth it for the magnificent views.

Park in the Breakwater Country Park and find the path that runs alongside the coast. You will see a plaque to the US airmen killed in 1944 on your right. Up the steep path to the top and then downhill to a junction where you bear left. Again left up a narrower path. Near a signpost, left again and up a steep path.

At the junction half way up the slope, bear left. At the next junction, left again and up the slope (not along the slope). Through the gap in the wall and follow the footpath to the top where there are the remains of a building. On the way up you will have a magnificent view of Holyhead Breakwater and port on your left and South Stack (Ynys Lawd) lighthouse on your right.

Follow the footpath down and then left at the junction following the path that runs alongside a wall and then downhill until you come to a crossroads (or crosspaths!) at the bottom of the slope. Straight ahead and up the steep slope on the left side of a large rock to the top and follow the path going straight ahead towards some rocks and to the highest point on Mynydd (Holyhead Mountain) with its obelisk, cairn and remains of an old Roman watchtower.

Have a breather here and look around at the wonderful views. Take the path straight ahead of you and go downhill. When you reach a junction, go straight ahead (not left) and then left down a well-defined path and then onto a track by a locked gate on your right. Carry on until you reach a waste patch of land, turn left along a concrete track to a gap to the right of a gate and into a small car park.

Go left along a well-defined path until you see about six large stones on your right and follow the path on your right just after the stones. Follow the track downhill and then go left when you reach the road. You will eventually see a chapel on your right and then a lane to *your left. Go up the lane past a large workshop on your right. Up the hill, and after a tight bend keep right going past Bryn Awelon on your right. Then at the bottom of the hill past a large house with garage on your right.*

Keep along the lane until you come to a cluster of houses. Past a house called Yeovil on your right and onto a footpath. Keep right and go downhill between gorse bushes with the breakwater in front of you. Then down several flights of steps and back to the Breakwater Park.

PLACES OF INTEREST

Breakwater: At 1½ miles long it is the largest breakwater in Britain. It was built between 1845 and 1873 and cost £1,285,000. Over a thousand men were employed building the structure, with more than 40 losing their lives.

Breakwater Country Park: The park is located on the site of the quarry that supplied about seven million tons of stone to construct the Holyhead Breakwater. From 1890 to 1973, the site was used for making bricks. It has been a country park since 1990. Signs of the tramway that was used to transport stone from the quarry along the breakwater during its construction can still be seen. The coastal footpath runs along this tramway for a while and can be followed up to the quarries.

Caergybi (Holyhead): The Romans built a stronghold in Caergybi in the 4th century which might have been rebuilt by Cadwallon Law Hir a hundred years later. The following century, Saint Cybi arrived to build a monastery which survived until the 13th century although Vikings attacked a couple of centuries earlier.

Due to its position as an excellent port to Ireland the settlement prospered. During the 17th century it was used to ferry troops over to Ireland to suppress the insurrections there and because of the situation in Ireland, the port was a centre for espionage and gathering intelligence. Passports were needed and checked and troops kept watch on any suspicious goings on.

The Irish were not the only visitors to Caergybi during the 17th century. It is said that during this time that Arab pirates attacked the town and captured over a 100 people for the white slave markets of northern Africa.

The ferry service to Ireland dates back to at least the 17th century. During the 18th century there were three packet-boats crossing to Dublin every week, taking sometimes about 12 hours to cross (compared to 1½ today). Before a pier was built, passengers were carried ashore by porters. The port was a hive of shipbuilding activity in the 18th and 19th centuries. Ships of up to 200 tons could be accommodated in the port and vessels from all over the west coast came here to be repaired.

The fishing quay lies largely empty today although at one time it was very important. In the early part of the 20th century, herring boats from the Isle of Man and Scotland came here to land their catches. The fish were then taken by rail to all over Europe.

Cytiau'r Gwyddelod at Porth Dafarch: Here are three Neolithic barrows which are examples of a cemetery which has been in use for over two or three hundred years, possibly by successive generations of the same small community who would have lived by farming and fishing They were heavily disturbed during the Roman period when groups of huts were built over them. They were entirely removed during the 19th century and a road built over them.

Cytiau Gwyddelod Tŷ Mawr: These were first excavated in the 1860s by WO Stanley MP of Penrhos and the site is one of Anglesey's best known early settlements. Much excavation was also done in the 1970s and 1980s. There is evidence of occupation here from as early as the Middle Stone Age (10,000BC). The buildings here today have been identified as belonging to the Iron Age. On the site are ten hut circles, the wall base of circular houses, other rectangular partly underground buildings (which were probably workshops) and evidence of fields. Materials found at the site suggest that this area was occupied as recently as the 6th century, at the time of Saint Cybi.

Elin's Tower: The tower was built as a summer house in 1868 by WO Stanley for his daughter Elin. After falling into disrepair in the 1930s, the tower was bought and restored by the Royal Society for the Protection of Birds in the 1980s. It now provides spectacular views through a large window and via a closed circuit camera attached to the cliffside. In early summer guillemots, razorbills, puffins and gulls can be seen nesting on ledges on the cliff face.

Lifeboat: A lifeboat was established in Holyhead in 1828, the second on Ynys Môn. A steam lifeboat was stationed here in 1890 with the first motor lifeboat arriving in 1922. It remains one of the main lifeboat stations in the area. Over a period of 150 years, Holyhead lifeboats saved over 1300 lives. There was also a lifeboat at Porth Ruffydd to the south-west of Caergybi between 1891 and 1903.

In the Maritime Museum in the old Lifeboat House are details of the ill-fated *Tara*, which used to be the ferry *Hibernia* travelling from Caergybi to Ireland but which was requisitioned during the First World War. In November 1915 it was torpedoed in the Mediterranean by a German submarine. The crew of 93 (many from Caergybi) took to the boats and reached the African coast where they spent months in the desert before being rescued

Mynydd Twr: Some of the oldest rocks in Britain are found in Anglesey and here Pre-Cambrian strata forms the highest point on the island. On the summit is a Prehistoric hill fort called Caer y Twr with an area of about seven hectares enclosed by a stone rampart over three metres high in places. Due to its excellent position, in the 4th century the Romans built a watch tower on the site. Roman coins have been found here.

Also on the mountain, there used to be a semaphore signal station which was one of eleven built in the 1800s to give Liverpool merchants early warning of the approach of their ships. These were relayed down the line by the wooden arms of the masts.

Nicholas Monserrat died 8 August 1979 in London. His most famous novel is probably *The Cruel Sea* written in 1951. It is one of the classic novels of the Second World War – the story of the Battle of the Atlantic, the struggle between the German U-boats and the British merchant fleet and the battles those navies fought with the cruel sea.

Porth Dafarch: Between 1819 and 1820 this is where the ferries to Ireland left. It was also used later when adverse winds in Holyhead harbour made it inaccessible.

The four-masted screw barque *SS Missouri* lies in pieces on the sea bed off here. In February 1886 she was sailing from Boston, USA, to Liverpool with a mixed cargo of live cattle, hides, palm oil and cotton bales. A south-westerly gale blew the ship in dense fog and a snowstorm onto the shore. The crew tried to lighten the load by sending overboard a quarter of the 395 cattle, but the crew eventually had to abandon ship. Only 50 of the cattle were saved. Some of the cargo was recovered but not before looters had been there and several men were tried and convicted of theft.

St Cybi's Church: St Cybi is believed to have lived in the 6th century. He was a great traveller having been on a pilgrimage to Jerusalem. On returning to Wales, he travelled with four disciples – Maelog, Llibio, Peulan and Cyngar – and was given land by Maelgwyn on Ynys Cybi (Holy Island). The present St Cybi's Church is partly 12th century, surrounded by a wall dating back to the 4th century.

Caergybi means Cybi's fort. It is enclosed on three sides and originally stood on the edge of the slope above the sea. The style of the masonry, its position and plan have led it to it being dated as late Roman. The later church built inside is said to have been granted to Cybi in the 6th century, although the earliest surviving evidence is from the 12th century. A second church inside the fort, Eglwys y Bedd (Church of the Grave), may mark the site of the saint's grave.

According to legend, St Cybi used to meet St Seiriol from Penmon at Llannerch-y-medd very week. Because Seiriol always walked with his face away from the sun he became Siriol Wyn (white-faced) while Cybi, always walking towards the sun, became Cybi Felyn (tanned).

South Stack lighthouse: A petition to build a lighthouse on Ynys Lawd was first made to Charles II in 1665 but it was not until 1809 that a lighthouse was established here. The lighthouse cost £12,000 to build and was originally fitted with oil lamps and reflectors. But fog often obscured the light so, in 1840, a perpendicular rail was installed so that a lantern giving extra light could be lowered down to sea level. A new lantern was installed in the mid 1870s and in 1909 an incandescent mantle burner. Electricity was used from 1938 onwards. The lighthouse became automated in 1984 and the light and fog signal are now remotely controlled from Harwich in Essex.

There is a deep gorge between Ynys Lawd and Ynys Cybi which was originally traversed by a hemp cable about twenty yards above sea level along which a sliding basket was drawn carrying the keepers and stores. This was replaced by a suspension bridge in 1828 and by an aluminium bridge in 1964. The present footbridge was installed in 1997.

The lighthouse is now a listed building and open to the public. There are over 300 steps leading down to the suspension bridge.

In 1900 the barque *Primrose Hill* was wrecked south of here on her way from Liverpool to Australia. She was caught in a north-west gale, her sails were torn and with her anchors dragging she struck submerged rocks and broke up with the loss of 33 lives.

SS Castilian: She was a steamship freighter which sank in February 1943. She sailed from Manchester for Lisbon and was wrecked during the wartime blackout after waiting to join a southbound convoy. She ran onto West Platters reef near the

Skerries. On board was 40mm Beaufor guns, heavy machine-gun bullets, anti-aircraft shells (many are still intact and live and scattered around the wreck!), aircraft propeller blades, POW mail and copper ore. The Royal Navy has made attempts at salvaging the ammunition but large amounts still remain on the sea bed.

Ynys Arw (North Stack): A fog station opened here in 1857. The keepers used donkeys to carry food and explosives along the narrow winding path for the fog warning gun which is now kept in the Breakwater Country Park after being recovered from the bottom of the cliffs in 1984.

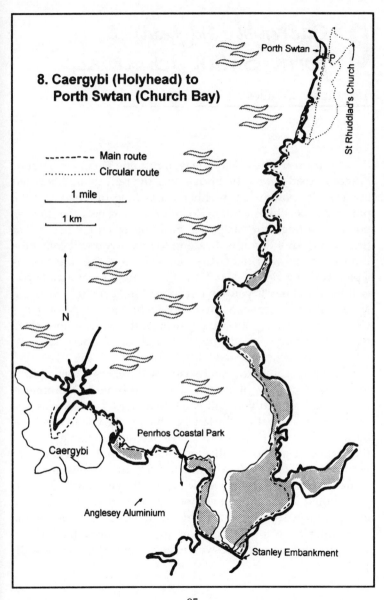

8. Caergybi (Holyhead) to Porth Swtan (Church Bay)

Porth Swtan

P

St Rhuddlad's Church

- - - - - - - Main route
.... Circular route

1 mile

1 km

N

Caergybi

Penrhos Coastal Park

Anglesey Aluminium

Stanley Embankment

8 Caergybí (Holyhead) to Porth Swtan (Church Bay)

5 ½ hours – 15 miles

Park your car by the side of the wall running along the harbour (Victoria Road), cross the bridge over the railway and bear left towards the port. You can either walk along the road past the port car parks (Turkey Shore Road) or walk as near the shore as possible through the car parks until you reach the South Pier (the Fish Quay). If you walk along the road you will come to a timber yard on your right. As soon as you pass the yard there is a path running alongside it. If the tide is in, this is the route you will have to take. If you have reached the Fish Quay, you will see a wall approximately three foot high; you can go over this wall onto the shore, but if the tide is in, the water comes up to the wall and you would have to walk on slippery seaweed which is not recommended.

Before reaching the quay you will see to your right a monument on top of a hill, this is **Skinner's Monument.** Following the path you will come to a factory, as soon as you pass it, there is a path to the left which will take you to the shore, more or less where you would have been if you had gone over the wall. You can now walk along the beach but there are signs warning you to keep a look out for the ferries for they sometimes create large waves which reach the shore and can be dangerous. Walk along Penrhos Beach with a hospital and aluminium works on your right. At the end of the beach you will either have to clamber over rocks or follow the cliff-top footpath, and in some cases you have no choice but to follow the path.

You will now reach **Penrhos Coastal Park,** and by the flagpole there is a Falklands War Memorial. Further along is the **Tollhouse Cafe.** You will now reach the Stanley Embankment; you cannot walk alongside it the whole length, therefore you will have to walk on it. When you reach the end of the wall on your left hand side, before reaching the tyre depot, turn left down onto the beach.

Walk along the shore passing the old fish weir **Gorad Alaw** on your left. You will then reach the estuary of river Alaw. If the tide is out, you can walk through the mud, crossing a couple of shallow streams, right across the estuary (be careful when the tide comes in!). If the tide is in, you will have to walk inland along the shore which adds another frustrating mile and a half to your journey. For the first half of the journey you will see the Holyhead port and breakwater and **Anglesey Aluminium's** tall chimney to your left.

Carry on along the shore which has some sandy patches, but is mostly pebbly and in some places rocky. You will pass Porth Tywyn Mawr, Porth Defaid, Porth Trefadog, Porth Trwyn until you reach Porth Tyddyn Uchaf where a large headland juts out into the sea. It is impossible to follow the shore unless it is a very low tide and you like rock-climbing, so its is advisable to join the path running along the headland (if you don't like walking along the pebbly/rocky shore you can follow this path from just after the Alaw estuary).

On your right you will see a dried stream bed (unless it's been raining!). Go up this towards a pipe opening and you will have reached the path. Turn left through the kissing-gate and along the path. Follow this path until you get to **Porth Swtan.** As you reach Porth Swtan you can see the lighthouse on Ynysoedd y Moelrhoniaid (Skerries) to your left, ahead of you the church spire of **St Rhuddlad** which gives the bay its English name and to your left the thatched roof of **Bwthyn Swtan.** The path is above the beach of Porth Swtan and you have to walk down a lane to the beach, which takes less than a minute. In

Porth Swtan is north Wales' premier fish restaurant, The Lobster Pot. There is also a cafe, car park and toilets.

CIRCULAR ROUTE

1 or 1½ hours – 3 or 5 miles

Park you car in the Porth Swtan (Church Bay) car park near the toilets. You might like to visit Bwthyn Swtan before you start your journey. Leave the car park and walk downhill until you come to a cafe. Turn left, through two kisisng-gates, and along the coastal path to Porth Penrhyn with its white cottage. Proceed along the coastal path. You will come to some concrete steps and footbridge. Don't go over the stile on your left, but when the tide is out you can go down the gully on your right to the beach and walk along it.

Otherwise, walk along the coastal path. After passing a cluster of houses on your left, go down the path on your right to the beach at Porth Trwyn. Just after the house on the edge of the beach at the far end you will see a path going inland to a road. Turn left here and go along the road. You will eventually see an old wildmill to your right.

Downhill to a junction. Now you can either go down to Porth Swtan (Church Bay) car park which is a few minutes away or carry on along the road and up the hill where there are magnificent views. If you choose the second option, go along the road, downhill, then uphill past the Church Bay Inn on your right and then St Rhwydrus' Church on your left.

Just before the church, you will see a footpath sign. Go up the track to the top of the hill. You will see a footpath to your left over a stile. Here there are wonderful views of Porth Swtan (Church Bay) and the coast and Mynydd Twr (Holyhead Mountain) ahead of you. Follow the footpath down the fields towards the sea until you reach the coastal path which takes you back to the Porth Swtan car park.

PLACES OF INTEREST

Anglesey Aluminium: The aluminium smelter was opened in

1970 on a 30 acre site. Telford's road had to be diverted and a new jetty was built in the harbour from where a tunnel under the town carries raw materials to the plant on a conveyor belt.

Bwthyn Swtan: The last thatched cottage on Ynys Môn stands near the shore of Porth Swtan. It is owned by the National Trust but has been leased to the Friends of Swtan, a local conservation group.

Gorad Alaw: It is a stone fish weir, some four feet thick, at the mouth of river Alaw. Originally it was higher but the action of the tides have reduced it in size. The weir stretches across the mouth of the river but at low water there is a 20 foot gap between its end and the shore. The tide would bring fish past the weir, but – due to the nature of the currents – the fish would be caught with the water escaping back to the sea. Originally the stones would have oak posts and willow weave between them and the trapped fish would be caught in nets. Shipbuilding flourished here during the 18th century.

Penrhos – on land owned by Anglesey Aluminium, it became a nature reserve in the 1970s. It previously belonged to the Penrhos estate. At the entrance is a Falklands War Memorial. The broad flats of Beddmanarch Bay near the reserve are feeding grounds for geese and wading birds

Porth Swtan (Church Bay): Swtan is Welsh for whiting (a fish) but since the spire of Llanrhuddlad Church was so prominent from the sea, a marine chart of 1816 called it Church Bay

Skinner's Monument – was erected in memory of John Macgregor Skinner who was born in America about 1760. He saw many years' service at sea, and lost an arm during the American War of Independence and a right eye in 1780. He then joined the Post Office and came to Caergybi to command a packet-boat sailing to Dublin. For 32 years he was an outspoken critic of the management of the postal service, complaining that the ships were badly constructed and that huge fares and poor accommodation for passengers were losing the town valuable trade. Skinner was returning from Dublin on the packet boat

Escape in October 1832 when, a short distance from port, large waves struck the ship and broke into the bulwark where he was standing, and he was swept out to sea. A few days later his body was seen, fully dressed, in the water near Ynys Lawd. The following day it was found in Porth Dafarch, headless and naked.

St Rhuddlad's Church: Rhuddlad was the daughter of the King of Leinster in Ireland, whose feast is on the 4th of September. The present church was built in 1858 and unusually for Anglesey it has a spire.

Stanley Embankment (o'r Cob as it's known locally), designed by Thomas Telford as part of the Holyhead Turnpike Road (later known as the A5), is 1300 yards long and 16 feet above high water. It was opened in 1822 – four years before Pont y Borth (Menai Suspension Bridge). It is named after William Stanley, the Liberal MP for the island between 1837-74, whose family owned the land over which the post road passed. The rubble for the embankment was stored in an excavated valley near a cluster of houses called Tŷ Coch, which eventually became known as Valley. The embankment was widened in the 1960s during the construction of the Anglesey Aluminium smelter nearby to carry water pipes from the Alaw reservoir to the works and electricity along cables from the nuclear power station at Yr Wylfa. Before building the embankment, apart from going through Pont-rhydbont, the only other route was along the sands to the north.

Toll House: A number of toll houses were built alongside the Holyhead Turnpike Road to collect money from those using it. This one at Penrhos has been converted into a cafe run by a local charity.

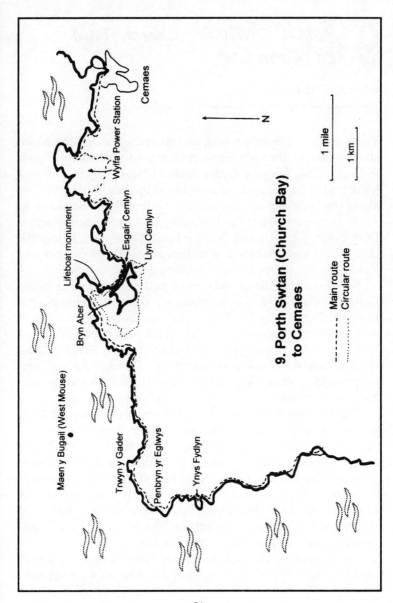

9. Porth Swtan (Church Bay) to Cemaes

- - - - - Main route
.... Circular route

Cemaes

Wylfa Power Station

Lifeboat monument

Bryn Aber

Esgair Cemlyn

Llyn Cemlyn

Maen y Bugail (West Mouse)

Trwyn y Gader

Penbryn yr Eglwys

Ynys Fydlyn

N

1 mile
1 km

9 Porth Swtan (Church Bay) to Cemaes

6 hours – 11 miles

There are two possible routes on this stage – along the rocky shore as far as Trwyn y Crewyn then onto the headland path until you pass **Trwyn y Gader (Carmel Head)** (which means a lot of scrambling over rocks and should be done at low tide), or along the coastal path. If you take the first route, go down to Porth Swtan and walk northwards past Ogof Lowri, Porth y Dwr, Porth y Bribys and Porth y Nant. Otherwise, follow the path to the right (which is a continuation of the one that you arrived on above Porth Swtan), which starts above the bay.

Follow the headland route until you reach a ravine called Gwter Fudur. Here is a sign saying that it's a 'permissive footpath' but nearby is a sign saying 'no footpath'. Anyway, it seems that it is possible to walk along the path. When you come to a large stile, do not go over it but keep to the left of it along the headland until you come to a track. Through the gate and keep walking along the path to another stile and down towards **Ynys Fydlyn** with the marshy Llyn Fydlyn to your right.

The land from here is private, but you are allowed to walk along the path apart from between 14 September and 1 February. Up to a kissing-gate and onto the National Trust's Mynachdy land with **Ynysoedd y Moelrhoniaid (Skerries)** to your left. Walk along the path past **Penbryn yr Eglwys** towards Trwyn y Gader (Carmel Head). Here there is a ruin with traces of excavation, a tall chimney and two white markers (known as the **White Ladies**) to your right. To your left is **Maen y Bugail (West Mouse)** with another white marker.

Over a stone style with a notice to keep to the coastal path which we intend to do anyway! You will then reach an old mine shaft with a warning to keep out. The path along here is very difficult to follow but walk as near to the edge as possible, keeping out of the farmer's hay. To your right is the old church of **St Rhwydrus** which is worth a detour. Back to the headland and follow the path until you come to a **monument** noting the 150th anniversary of the establishing of the **first lifeboat** on Ynys Môn. Past the ruins of **Bryn Aber** on your right and onto the beach running alongside Esgair Cemlyn. As you approach here during early summer, you will hear the crying of numerous birds. Llyn Cemlyn, the other side of the pebbled bank, is a nature reserve and nesting area for terns.

Walk along the pebbly beach to a small car park and follow the official coastal path. Over a style with a sign 'Bull in Field' on it, but I didn't see one although I kept a sharp lookout and worked out my getaway route in case I saw one! Along the path and down to a pebbly beach until you reach **Wylfa Power Station.** You will reach a sign saying that it is a 'nuclear registered site'. Although it doesn't say 'keep out' you cannot go much further as there is a security fence and further along a sign saying that you can go no further! Don't try it – there might be armed guards there and you could start glowing in the dark!

Turn right and walk along the wall enclosing the power station until you come to a gate near some pine trees. Through the gate and onto the road by the power station entrance. Walk along the road until you come to the visitors' centre, cafe and nature trails. After a well-earned cuppa, out of the power station and turn left along a lane. Walk along it until you see a small car park on your right and a large pair of gates ahead of you. To the left of these gates is a kissing-gate. Through it and follow the track, not the footpaths, upwards until you come to a field. Keep to the left of the field and walk to the headland with the power station to your left. You are now more or less where you were before you had to make a detour around the power station.

Either follow the shore or the coastal path. You will eventually reach the outskirts of Cemaes. You will reach a sign saying Ponc y Môr Village Green. You cannot follow the shore here as the sea reaches to the rocks. Walk up to Anwylfa Residential Home and there is a path to your right which takes you to the beach at **Cemaes.**

CIRCULAR ROUTE
3 miles – 1 hour
Go to the car park on the left hand side (western side) of Cemlyn Nature Reserve near Bryn Aber. Walk towards the beach along the track, through a gap near a gate and you will reach the monument that commemorates the 150th anniversary of launching the first lifeboat on Ynys Môn. Wylfa Power Station is on your right. Then follow the path to the left to the shore.

Over a stile and walk along the edge of the field uphill to a kissing-gate. Again along the edge of the field to another kissing-gate. You will now see Ynysoedd y Moelrhoniaid (The Skerries) and the flashing lighthouse out at sea to your right.

Then downhill to another kissing-gate and down to where there is a gate going to the beach. Turn left, inland, along a path that runs along the side of a fence towards a farmhouse. Through the gate and left onto a lane. Walk past the lagoons on your left to a junction and then turn right. At the next junction, near a National Trust sign, go left and uphill past a farmhouse.

Then downhill to a Give Way sign. Go left here. At the junction near the white house on your left, don't turn right but go straight ahead until you come to a small car park near the beach. You turn left here. Either walk along the pebbly beach or walk along the footpath that runs alongside the lake. During the nesting season, you will have to walk along the beach.

When you reach a building you will have to cross a stream over a concrete embankment. Either go left along the rocks skirting the wall (which may be difficult at high tide) or go around the building to your right and then back into the car park where you started from.

PLACES OF INTEREST

Bryn Aber: The former home of millionaire Captain Vivian Hewitt. He was a passionate bird watcher and egg collector and built the weir at Cemlyn to form a lagoon. The purpose of the high walls around the house was to protect the trees and garden from the salt-laden winds and thus provide a bird sanctuary. He was also a pioneer aviator and made the first flight from Britain to Ireland in 1912. During the Second World War there were rumours that he was supplying German U-boats with fuel and he was investigated, but the tanks on his land only contained water. He died in 1965 and his land was bought by the National Trust.

Cemaes – is a medieval town and the former location of one of the courts of the Welsh princes, then called Castell Iorwerth after Prince Iorwerth. More recently, it was an important port and shipbuilding centre. It was also used for fishing, where herring was caught in huge quantities and salted. The harbour was improved in 1828, a slipway was added and a lifeboat station established in 1872. In the 19th century the port was used to export lime, limestone, ochre and marble, but this declined with the coming of the railway. Small schooners were built here in the 19th century.

Maen y Bugail (West Mouse): In 1823 the sailing packet *Alert* was driven by a strong tide onto these rocks. The ship was holed and sank and only seven of the 147 passengers and crew were rescued. Only 27 bodies were recovered, and they were buried in Caergybi (Holyhead). The rector of nearby Llanfair-yng-Nghornwy, James Williams, and his young wife Frances watched helpless from the shore. They eventually persuaded the newly-formed National Lifeboat Institution to provide a boat to be stationed in Cemlyn. They later founded the Ynys Môn branch of the RNLI. James Williams became a cox of the lifeboat and helped to save numerous lives. He later received the Gold Medal of the RNLI for saving the lives of five people in Cemaes Bay, not in a lifeboat but by riding his horse into the sea. There is a monument to them before reaching Cemlyn.

Penbryn yr Eglwys: There is evidence here of a small church founded in the 6th or 7th century. Later the site may have become a fort.

St Rhwydrus' Church: The nave and font of this simple church, which is situated in the middle of a field, are 12th century while the chancel was added a century later. There are a number of interesting gravestones in the churchyard, including one belonging to a Norwegian captain whose vessel was wrecked at Cemlyn in 1869.

Trwyn y Gader (Carmel Head): In November 1890 the Swedish sailing ship *Hudiksvall* was on her way from New York to Liverpool when she aimed for Caergybi (Holyhead) to shelter from strong winds. But her anchor did not hold and she was driven towards Carmel Head. Holyhead lifeboat was launched but when it reached the ship it had two broken masts with the crew hanging onto them. The lifeboat crew threw a rope and the crew of 16 were able to scramble to safety as their ship broke up and sank.

White Ladies – two beacons that align with the one on Maen y Bugail and which were built to help shipping go around Trwyn Cemlyn.

Wylfa Nuclear Power Station: Construction began in 1963 and reactor number one started generating electricity on January 1971 with reactor number two starting six months later. During construction, up to 3,000 men were employed here. It has a permanent staff of around 600 producing 23mKWH ef electricity – enough to meet the needs of two cities the size of Liverpool.

Ynysoedd y Moelrhoniaid (Skerries): The islands of the seals, a cluster of rocks with a lighthouse on one of them. They were given the name Skerries by the Vikings. It is on the important shipping route to Liverpool. In 1881 the sailing vessel *Gilbert Thompson* was under tow on the last part of her journey between Calcutta and Liverpool. As the ships were negotiating the channel between Ynysoedd y Moelrhoniaid and Maen y Bugail (West Mouse), the *Gilbert Thompson* keeled over in the strong tide and her iron hull was torn on jagged underwater rocks. The crew of 22, except a cabin boy with a broken leg, managed to scramble to safety on the rocks before the vessel sank. The men were rescued by the tug and taken to Liverpool.

The most important vessel to perish on these rocks was Charles, Pretender to the English throne's royal yacht, *Mary*. She was employed to carry important passengers between Ireland and England. In March 1675 she capsized near the rocks but her long mainmast touched the shore and 39 passengers and crew were able to reach safety, but 36 lost their lives including the Earl of Meath. The *Mary's* bronze guns were found by divers in 1971 and are now in the Maritime Museum in Liverpool along with coins, jewellery, tableware and even a woman's skeleton.

The rock on which the lighthouse stands is at the end of a strip of submerged land which is directly in the path of the major shipping lanes to Liverpool. The first lighthouse was coal-fired and established in 1714. Originally it was a private venture but it was bought by Trinity House in 1841. It was converted to electricity in 1927 and to automatic operation in 1987.

According to legend a smuggler came across two small boys adrift in a boat near here on a stormy night. One child died but the other was taken ashore and to a house called Mynachdy, the home of a Dr Lloyd. The boy was given the name Evan; it was believed he was Spanish as he had no Welsh or English. As he grew up (he had by now been given the surname Thomas), it was noticed that he had great skill in setting bones after he mended the broken leg of a chicken, and his reputation spread all over Ynys Môn. Within a generation there were 21 members of his family who were either doctors or bonesetters. His grandson – another Evan – set up in practice in Liverpool and his son, Hugh Owen Thomas, again a doctor, devised surgical instruments and what became known as the 'Thomas splint'. His surgery became known as the birthplace of modern orthopaedic surgery. On your way to or from Porth Swtan you will see a plaque on the gable-end of a house which says that Richard Evans, son of the boy found in the boat, lived there.

Ynys y Fydlyn: At one time a series of telegraph poles ran down the hillside carrying wires linking Ynysoedd y Moelrhoniaid with Ynys Môn. It is claimed that the Vikings once landed here.

10. Cemaes to Porth Amlwch

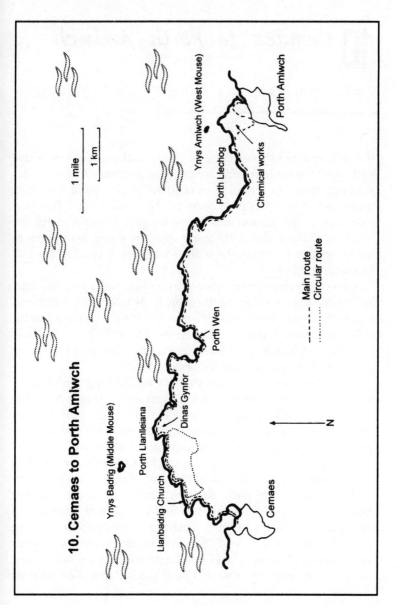

N

Ynys Badrig (Middle Mouse)

Porth Llanlleiana

Dinas Gynfor

Llanbadrig Church

Cemaes

Porth Wen

Porth Llechog

Chemical works

Ynys Amlwch (West Mouse)

Porth Amlwch

1 mile
1 km

----- Main route
.... Circular route

10 Cemaes to Porth Amlwch

9 miles – 5 hours

If you're coming by car there is ample parking space near the harbour. This route mainly follows the Anglesey Coastal Path although you can scramble over rocks on the shore here and there. Either take the path onto the National Trust's Trwyn y Parc land at the eastern end of the car park or walk along the beach. If walking along the beach there are a couple of paths at the far end up to the coastal path as you cannot proceed around Llanbadrig Point.

Carry on along the cliff path which takes you down to Porth Padrig. You can walk along the shore if the tide is out, otherwise return to the cliff path. You will now be able to see **Ynys Badrig (Middle Mouse)** out at sea. Along the cliff path towards **Llanbadrig Church.** You can either visit the church or follow the path which runs alongside the seaward wall.

You will now reach two paths. One running alongside a fence and another lower down. If you don't have a head for heights, I would strongly suggest the upper path. The lower path is very narrow with nothing between you and a steep precipice down to the sea. One slip – and it's the end!

Along either path until you reach **Porth Llanlleiana** and its ruined china clay works. Down into the bay and up the steep path. Along the cliff path, past the remains of an old **summer house** and on to **Dinas Gynfor.** Still on the path, down into Porth Cynfor (Hell's Mouth). Then up a steep path and along the cliff path to Torllwyn. You can scramble over the rocks nearer the sea in some places but the path is only about 20 yards from the sea anyway. You will now reach **Porth Wen** with its impressive ruined brick works. It is certainly worth going down the path to explore, but unfortunately you cannot walk from the harbour to the sandy beach to your right. You have to walk back along the path to rejoin the cliff path. It is virtually impossible to get down to the beach, but if you want to attempt it, try in winter when there is much less undergrowth!

Along the cliff path and follow a track that takes you inland until you reach a gate and stile. Across the field to another stile and follow the cliff path to a large white farmhouse. The path goes round the house, then up a farm track until you see a footpath sign pointing left. Follow the path back to the cliff edge and on to **Porth Llechog (Bull Bay).** Along this bit it is possible to scramble over rocks on the water's edge. You will reach a white house where it is not possible to follow the shore; you will therefore have to follow a path to your right to a kissing-gate and either down to the shore if the tide is out or carry on along the footpath to Porth Llechog beach.

Along the beach and either scramble over the rocks or walk along the pavement. There are deep creeks here and you will have to return to the pavement here and there, but as there as so many 'private' signs on gates leading into the bit of land, I doubt if it is worth the effort as the pavement runs a few yards from the shore.

You will then reach a small car park with the entrance to Porth Llechog (Bull Bay) **Golf Club.** Follow the path, scrambling over the rocks where possible, as far as the **chemical works** where you can see **Ynys Amlwch (West Mouse)** to your left. You cannot proceed along the coast here. Look for a path running inland about a 100 yards from and parallel to the works perimeter fence. Along a track, past a well, and onto another track until you see a stile on your left. Follow the path across a field aiming for some old containers on your left and out through a gate by the chemical works entrance. Turn right and go along the road around a football pitch, aiming for an old windmill. Up the track and down a footpath into **Porth**

Amlwch. Walk along the quayside towards the town.

If you intend carrying on to Walk 11, you will see a path turning down to your left by a housing estate so that you can go to the other side of the harbour. If you are making your way back along the main road you will go past the **windfarm, Rhosgoch** and **Mynydd Parys** from which Porth Amlwch owes its existence.

CIRCULAR ROUTE
4 miles – $1\frac{1}{2}$ hours

Make your way towards Llanbadrig Church. On entering Cemaes from the east, immediately after passing the sign, you will see signs on your right to The Gadlys Hotel and Llanbadrig Church. Follow the signs to Llanbadrig Church where you will find a small car park. You can either visit the church before starting the walk and joining the footpath by walking through the churchyard to a style or look for the coastal footpath sign to the left of the church.

On reaching the cliff edge, follow the path to your right along the churchyard wall, then right and over a stile. Now follow the cliff top path. Although this path is not dangerous, I would not recommend it to anyone who has no head for heights. In some places there are more than one path, especially on the headland opposite Ynys Badrig (Middle Mouse island), choose the one higher up which runs alongside a wall. The ones lower down near the cliff face are pretty hairy!

The path takes you eventually down to Porth Llanlleiana and its old brickworks. Spend a few minutes on the beach, then follow the path that runs inland. But if you fancy a further walk along the shore, go up the steep path towards Dinas Gynfor and eventually Borthwen before retracing your steps back to Porth Llanlleiana. This will add about another five miles to your journey.

From Porth Llanlleiana, walk inland along the footpath, then right over an embankment, through a gate, then follow the footpath alongside the edge of field. When you come to a farm gate and track, keep to the edge of the field on your right and aim for the corner of the field where there is a kissing-gate.

Out onto a road and turn right. By the white house, don't turn right, but carry straight on to a cluster of houses and then uphill. Then downhill to the junction by white houses and turn right and walk uphill to the car park near Llanbadrig's Church where you started from.

PLACES OF INTEREST

Chemical works: The plant, owned by Great Lakes Chemicals, produces bromine which is extracted from sea water. The bromine used to be transported by rail, which you cross when walking into Amlwch, but now goes by road leading to numerous tailbacks.

Dinas Gynfor: This is a late prehistoric fort – the most northerly fortification in Wales – whose defence walls can be seen on the inland side. To the west is a natural harbour where there are the remains of a small 19th century china clay quarry. The watchtower here commemorates the coronation of Edward VII.

Llanbadrig Church: There was a religious cell here from early times, but the earliest part of the present church is the 14th century chancel arch. The church contains an early gravestone decorated with a crudely-carved wheel-cross above a simple linear cross. It is the northernmost church in Wales, and the only one dedicated to St Patrick. To the north of the church is Ffynnon Badrig. According to legend Patrick was shipwrecked on Ynys Badrig (Middle Mouse) and crossed to Anglesey where he sheltered in a cave (which is now below the churchyard) and in AD440 founded the church. The present church dates from the 14th century but was restored in the 19th with money provided by the 3rd Lord Stanley who was a Moslem. He insisted that the church should have some Islamic elements and this is to be seen in the blue coloured windows and tiles. The church contains the Icthus stone, which was found during restoration work. It is probably a standing stone to which

Christian symbols were added in the 7th-11th century. The church was restored in 1985 after being set alight by vandals.

Mynydd Parys: One of the largest and most productive copper mines in Europe. Copper was mined here as early as the Bronze Age and was revived in the mid 18th century. The busiest period was from 1760 to 1850 when thousands worked here. Old prints show wooden platforms projecting perilously over the edge with winding gear which raised and lowered buckets carrying ore to the surface.

Porth Amlwch - has been a shipping and ship building centre for hundreds of years. It was once described as 'one of the most important ports in Wales'. At one time the creek was known as Porth Cwch y Brenin (the creek of the king's boat) suggesting that it was once the berth of a revenue cutter. The natural harbour was enlarged 200 years ago to accommodate larger vessels to carry copper ore from Mynydd Parys. At one time there were copper smelters here to smelt the ore but these have been demolished by now. The bins for the copper ore are still there as are the chimneys of the old lime kilns which supplied the smelting works.

Porth Llanlleiana: According to legend, a female recluse founded a chapel here about the 6th or 7th century and excavations many years ago revealed female bones. The deserted ruins are from the 19th century china clay industry when clay was dug from the hillside and exported from the quay to make porcelain.

Porth Llechog (Bull Bay) – was once a busy fishing port with ships being built and repaired here during the 19th century. The area was once noted for its smuggling. At one time, steamers from Liverpool used to call at the northern end of the bay to land passengers and goods. The bay once had a pilot station and a lifeboat. Offshore is the wreck of *HMS Pansy*, a former Wallasey paddle steamer taken over by the Admiralty, which sank in a gale in 1916. The name Bull Bay comes from a deep pool on the shore called Pwll y Tarw (The Bull Pool).

Porth Wen: Here is an abandoned brickworks which closed during the Second World War. Quartzite from a quarry on the hill behind was sent down an incline to the brickworks where silica bricks were produced and exported from the quay to be used in the steel industry. But the large swell by the quay made it difficult to load ships and eventually the owners were refused insurance. The tall chimneys and kilns survive.

Roman Baths and Golf Club: The baths were built for the Third Marquess of Anglesey in 1864 with the intention of adding a house later on, but it was never built. The baths were cut out of the rock and surrounded by walls and towers. The baths, known locally as the Roman Baths, were cleaned and refilled by each tide. In 1913 the Sixth Marquess opened the golf club nearby.

Shell Marine Terminal: Built in Rhosgoch in 1973 at the same time as the modern breakwater, oil from a mooring buoy two miles offshore was pumped ashore here and sent along an underground pipeline to the refinery at Stanlow, Cheshire. The terminal closed in 1987.

Summer House: This derelict building is a former summer-house of the Stanley family. It has an underfloor cavity – possibly to keep food and wine cool.

Ynys Amlwch (East Mouse): Between this island and the chemical works lies the wreck of the *Dakota*, a huge steamship which was sailing from Liverpool to New York in May 1877. She was a fast ship and was following a course about two miles offshore when, for some reason, she changed course which took her onto rocks. The crew and passengers were rescued by the Porth Llechog lifeboat.

Ynys Badrig (Middle Mouse): According to legend a missionary called Padrig was shipwrecked here who then crossed onto Ynys Môn and found shelter in a cave, below the churchyard in Llanbadrig, which was founded in AD440.

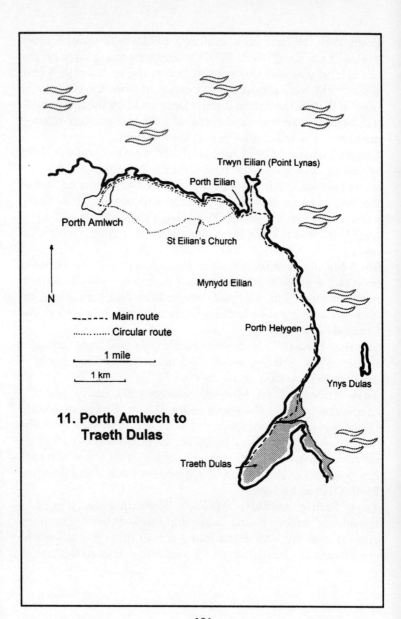

Trwyn Eilian (Point Lynas)

Porth Eilian

Porth Amlwch

St Eilian's Church

Mynydd Eilian

N

Porth Helygen

Main route
Circular route

1 mile

1 km

Ynys Dulas

11. Porth Amlwch to Traeth Dulas

Traeth Dulas

11 Porth Amlwch to Traeth Dulas

9 miles – 4 hours

Either, walk up from the harbour at Porth Amlwch up to the Heritage Museum, or if you're coming by car you can park just past the museum. Either follow the track and then path or scramble over the rocks from the harbour. After passing a large white house you will reach a creek where you have to walk on the path.

Then, either continue on the path, or scramble over the shore where possible until you reach Porth Eilian. Before reaching here, you can make a small detour inland towards **Ffynnon Eilian.** You can either return to the path or walk along the beach and if the tide is out scramble over the rocks at the far end towards **Trwyn Eilian (Point Lynas).** If you walk the path, you will reach a track and then a road towards Trwyn Eilian lighthouse. You can either follow the road along the middle of the promontory or walk along the cliff edge. Before you return to the cliff path, you can make a detour and visit **St Eilian's Church** in Llaneilian.

After walking around the lighthouse, either walk back along the road or along the cliff edge on the east shore, If returning along the road, you will come to a path on your left. Follow this cliff-top path. You can continue to scramble over the rocks in some places but when it becomes impossible it is sometimes very difficult to rejoin the path.

The path is sometimes very difficult to find due to the shoulder-high bracken, but here and there you will see marker-posts and stiles. Inland from Trwyn Du is **Mynydd Eilian** with its masts. From Trwyn Du it is possible to walk all the way along the rocks and pebbly beaches of Porth y Gwichiad and Porth Helygen.

I must admit when I followed the path I got lost in the bracken above Porth Helygen and found it much easier walking along the rocky shore than fighting through the vegetation. Carry on along the shore until you reach the sandy beach of **Traeth Dulas** with a large castellated house, Portobello, on the shore. Out at sea you will see an island with a tower on it – this is **Ynys Dulas.**

You can now either wade through Afon Goch which runs across the beach and proceed along Route 12 or walk along the shore by the side of the river towards the end of the bay where you will reach a track and then a lane that will take you to the A5025 where you can catch a bus back to Porth Amlwch.

CIRCULAR ROUTE
8½ miles – 2½ hours

Park your car in Llaneilian on the road that goes towards Porth Eilian. Out of the car park and left up the road, past the telephone kiosk and along the road to the right. Past St Eilian's Church on your left. Along the road downhill until you come to a cluster of houses.

Look for the footpath to your right just before Plas Heulog. Up the footpath, then left at the end of the gorse bushes to a kissing-gate and then right onto the road. Walk downhill into Porth Amlwch. By the Adelphi pub, turn right. You might like to visit the little harbour here or go straight up Upper Quay Street to the Heritage Centre where there is an exhibition and a cafe.

Then ahead to the car park and along the coastal path. After a while you will see the lighthouse on Trwyn Eilian. Carry on along the path, over stiles and footbridges and through kissing gates until you come to Porth Eilian. Up the slipway, then left up a hill and onto Trwyn Eilian. Walk up the promontory to the lighthouse. You cannot go in, but there are paths around it. Then retrace your steps to Porth Eilian and go up the road past toilets on your left to the car park where you started from.

PLACES OF INTEREST

Ffynnon Eilian: The spring is associated with the 7th century St Eilian who founded Llaneilian church. To bless the corn and cattle and for cures for ailments, prayers were said near the well and offerings were put into a *cyff* (chest) in Llaneilian church. It is also known as the cursing well with names of whoever you didn't like being scratched on small slates and thrown into the water.

Mynydd Eilian: A semaphore station was established here – the third from Ynys Cybi (South Stack) to Ynys Seiriol.

St Eilian's Church – is a medieval church with a simple twelfth century spire, thought to be the oldest in Wales. It has a painting of a skeleton on the rood screen with the message *Colyn Angau yw Pechod* (The sting of death is sin). There are also carved figures of minstrels with flutes and bagpipes in the chancel. There is a fine cross in the churchyard and at one time an ossuary which is said contained the bones of shipwrecked sailors. It is thought that there was an earlier church on this site. St Eilian was a sixth century saint who sailed from Rome with his family and landed at Porth yr Ychain. It is said that Eilian restored the sight of Prince Caswallon who, in thanks, gave him land. Here was one of the most important Gwyliau Mabsant (saints' days) or fairs with people from all over the island coming here on the first three Fridays in August. People, often drunk, would try and lie in Eilian's chest. If they succeeded to turn around in the confined space they would live a year longer! Another 'game' was to try and squeeze through a narrow division in a wooden panel in the church without touching the sides. If they succeeded, it would bring them good luck!

Traeth Dulas: There was once a thriving herring fishery here at one time and in the eighteenth century a flourishing shipbuilding industry.

Trwyn Eilian (Point Lynas) Lighthouse: It was built in 1835 to replace an earlier watchtower built in 1781. The lighthouse is different to most as it has a semicircular glass window with a static light rather than a revolving one. It is these days unmanned. At one time it was an important pilot station with pilots joining vessels to guide them into the busy port of Liverpool. There were up to six pilot boats here moored in the shelter of Porth Eilian.

One of the lost interesting people associated with the lighthouse was Robert Beaver who was born in Aberffraw in 1748. He went to sea at an early age and within a few years commanded his own ship. He traded in linens, woollens, cotton, sugar and slaves. In 1781 he received permission to attack and plunder Spanish ships in the West Indies. In three years he captured over 50 ships and amassed a great fortune. Because of ill health he returned to Anglesey and settled with his wife and 11 children at Maes y Llwyn, Amlwch, and took responsibility for the Trwyn Eilian Lighthouse.

Trwyn Eilian (Point Lynas) Telegraph house: Built in 1841 by the Trustees of Liverpool Dock, it was used to send messages along the coast that ships were on their way to Liverpool.

Ynys Dulas: A beacon was built here in 1824 to warn shipping and was paid for by Lady Dorina Neave of Llys Dulas. The tower has a shelter for shipwrecked sailors and was at one time stocked with food and water, firewood and brandy. Many ships were wrecked here including the schooner *Clagan* in 1917. The only survivors were the cabin boy and the ship's dog.

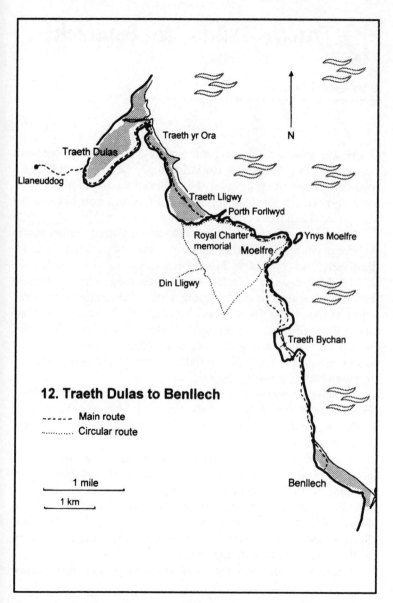

12. Traeth Dulas to Benllech

- - - - - - Main route
.... Circular route

1 mile

1 km

Traeth yr Ora

Traeth Dulas

Llaneuddog

Traeth Lligwy

Porth Forllwyd

Royal Charter memorial

Ynys Moelfre

Moelfre

Din Lligwy

Traeth Bychan

Benllech

N

12 Traeth Dulas to Benllech

9 miles – 4 hours

There are three way to start this journey. If the tide is out you can walk along the sands around Craig y Sais, if the tide is in you can follow the path over the promontory to Traeth yr Ora, or if in-between you can follow the shore but you have to be careful as it can be very wet.

If you are not continuing from Route 11, you can either leave your car near Traeth Dulas (a bit remote) or park your car in Benllech and take the bus northwards to the hamlet of Llaneuddog near City Dulas. At the crossroads, there is a road turning seawards towards Traeth Dulas, although there is no sign. At the end of the road, before reaching the beach, you will see a footpath sign to you right. Follow this if the tide is out which takes you across a footbridge. Now you can decide to either follow the footpath or make your way along the edge of the water after crossing the bridge.

Whichever route you take, you will reach Traeth yr Ora. From here, you can either walk along the shore or the clifftop footpath, depending on the tide, and along to Traeth Lligwy, were there's a shop.

The next part is a mixture of walking along small bays, scrambling over rocks or walking along the clifftop path. After passing **Porth Forllwyd,** on your right, you will see a small hill and on it the monument to those who lost their lives on the *Royal Charter.* You will then reach the **Moelfre Lifeboat Station,** then past Moelfre Seawatch, which is a 'life and history of the sea', and onto Moelfre beach.

Either scramble over the rocks at the far end of the beach or follow the road up a hill, past the anchor of the *Hindlea* which is on the left after you pass the shop by the car park. You will then see a footpath sign on your left which takes you down a lane and onto a footpath.

If you are following the footpath, you will reach a lane which takes you through a farm and car park and back onto the footpath. You will then arrive at the wide beach of **Traeth Bychan** where there is a shop. The footpath from here takes you inland to the A5025. After reaching the main road, turn left for about half a mile and then left to Pen-llain campsite following the footpath which takes you to the southern end of Traeth Bychan where you can follow the clifftop footpath.

Otherwise, walk along the coast, scrambling over large rocks, and as some are covered in seaweed, it's quite a struggle. In one or two places, when you have had enough of walking along the shore, you can scramble up the slope to the footpath. The footpath takes you to Traeth Benllech.

CIRCULAR ROUTE
7 miles – 2½ hours

Leave your car in either of the car parks above Moelfre (near the bus stop). Out of the car park and back in the direction you came from until you come to a junction, then right along the road and up the hill until you come to a roundabout. Turn right following the signs towards Din Lligwy and Traeth Lligwy. Follow this road until you see the sign on the left to the Lligwy Burial Chamber and a kissing-gate. Have a look at it.

Then back onto the road until you see the sign on the left to Din Lligwy. Over the stile and along the edge of the field following the path through two kissing-gates and through woodland until you reach the remains of a medieval village. Take your time to have a look around, then retrace your steps aiming for Capel Lligwy standing in the middle of the field. Then back along the edge of the field to the stile and back onto the road.

Turn left and follow the road until you come to a junction. Straight across and downhill to Traeth Lligwy car park. In summer, there is a shop here selling snacks. You can now either follow the path to your right behind the shop or go down to the beach. If going onto the beach, walk eastwards until you come to the end of the beach and you can rejoin the clifftop path by using the steps which go up the slope.

Along the clifftop path, through a kissing-gate, then right alongside a fence to another kissing-gate. Follow the footpath which runs alongside a high wall to another kissing-gate. After a while, just before a caravan park, you will see the monument to those who lost their lives when the Royal Charter sank. Further along, there is a stone stile and a path running up to the monument.

Back again to the clifftop path and to a kissing-gate which takes you into the caravan park. Keep to the left edge and walk towards another kissing-gate. The path then goes through thorn bushes. Over a stone stile to a kissing-gate and to open ground. Follow the path to your right aiming for some houses. Look for the signpost that guides you up the field to another kissing-gate. Turn left and through the gate before turning right along a lane past cottages on your left, then right and down towards the lifeboat station.

Then right and along the path that takes you past Moelfre Seawatch which you can visit and then onto the beach at Moelfre. Up the hill after passing the shop and car park. At the top of the hill, turn right towards the bus stop and then right into the car park from where you started.

PLACES OF INTEREST

Benllech: The original village expanded when the railway reached it in 1908 bringing tourists to the area, but the line closed to passengers in 1930 although goods were carried until 1950. Up to the arrival of the tourists, the main employers were the stone quarries which produced millstones and high quality black and grey marble for export, and fishing. The arrival of the train enabled fresh fish to be sent to markets in Chester,

Liverpool and Manchester.

Capel Lligwy or Hen Gapel: Here are the remains of a 12th century church. The nave and chancel were rebuilt in the 14th century. Inside the south chapel, which was added 200 years later, a flight of steps leads down to a small crypt.

Din Lligwy – is an enclosed hut group covering about half an acre, dating back to at least the Roman period. Excavations have revealed both earlier and later occupation. It was probably the home of an important local chieftain. The circular huts were houses where pottery, glassware and ingots have been found whilst the rectangular ones were workshops or barns. Iron smelting hearths have been found in some of the buildings.

Hindlea – a 500 ton coaster which was wrecked in October 1959. The empty cargo boat had been caught in a violent storm and was sheltering in Bae Dulas. The wind changed direction and the *Hindlea* started to drag anchor. The Moelfre lifeboat was summoned, but although the full crew was available, the regular boat was not. Nevertheless, the coxswain set out in hurricane force winds and 25 foot waves. The boat was skilfully manoeuvred towards the ship – eight times, with a member of the ship's crew jumping aboard each time. Shortly afterwards the ship smashed against the rocks and broke in two. For this dramatic rescue the lifeboat crew were awarded RNLI medals. The *Hindlea's* anchor can be seen behind the shop on the front at Moelfre.

Lligwy Burial Chamber – was built around 2500 – 2000BC. The tomb has a large stone weighing about 25 tons covering a chamber dug into the rock. It was excavated in 1909 and a number of remains of about 30 people were found with some items of pottery dating from the end of the Neolithic period.

Moelfre: At one time, Moelfre herring was renowned all over the island with fishermen's wives travelling to the various towns and villages to sell their product. Moelfre seamen used to travel the world on large ocean going ships, but would return to Moelfre for the herring season which began in October and lasted until February. The industry declined at the beginning of the Second World War.

Moelfre Lifeboat: The first lifeboat in Moelfre was established in 1909 to the north of the village; the previous station being established at Porth Nigwyl to the south of the village in 1875.

Porth Forllwyd: A small quay was built here during the nineteenth century to load stone onto trading sloops that sailed between Dublin, Anglesey and Liverpool.

Royal Charter: The luxury steam clipper was returning from Australia when, on 25 October 1859, was struck by hurricane strength winds which drove it onto the rocks, splitting it in two. This was the worst storm of the century. More than four hundred people drowned. Most of them were returning from the Australian gold fields and the ship was laden with gold – probably about £300,000 worth. Charles Dickens was sent to Moelfre to report on the tragedy and said that gold sovereigns were scattered on the beach. Only a small proportion of the gold was recovered by the receiver with stories that much of it found its way to the homes of the locals. The remains of the ship can be seen at low tides and objects are sometimes washed up onto the shore.

Thetis: The submarine *Thetis* was grounded near Traeth Bychan in 1939 after failing to surface during trials in Liverpool Bay. Ninety-nine crewmen lost their lives. The submarine was later towed away and served in the Second World War after being renamed *Thunderbolt*.

Traeth Bychan: At the northern end of the beach is a little harbour which at one time accommodated boats which carried millstone from the nearby quarry.

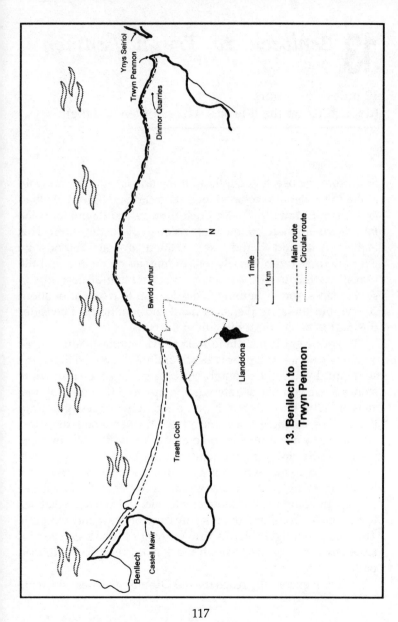

13. Benllech to Trwyn Penmon

N

1 mile

1 km

——— Main route
········· Circular route

Ynys Seiriol

Trwyn Penmon

Dinmor Quarries

Bwrdd Arthur

Llanddona

Traeth Coch

Benllech

Castell Mawr

13 Benllech to Trwyn Penmon

12 miles – 5-6 hours
(depending on the tide and which route you take)

Start from the beach at Benllech. If the tide is out you can walk along the water's edge on golden sands around Trwyn Dwlban and **Castell Mawr** to **Traeth Coch (Red Wharf Bay)** and to the far end where there are the remains of an old fishing weir. This is the easy bit and should take you about an hour. You now go over the rocks (with literally tons of mussels on them or in little pools) – a mixture of walking and scrambling at first, but in some places, some climbing is needed, up to a height of about 20 feet, but there are plenty of hand and foot holds. I consider this part to be the most difficult in the book.

To your right is the **Llanddona** television mast. You go past a quarry near a small pebbly beach and then carry on along the shore until you come to another pebbly beach covered in white stones. Here you will see steps going up the cliff to the National Trust's Fedw Fawr estate. I would strongly suggest going up these steps as there are some places further along the coast which are near-impossible to go along. You will have, by now, seen **Ynys Seiriol (Puffin Island)** ahead of you.

If you go up the steps, you will come to a small car park, bear left along a lane, past a house, around a corner and you will see a footpath going to your left along a field which takes you back to the coast. From here on, it's a mixture of coast and footpath. The coast, although a bit of a struggle over the rocks, can be a bit easier than struggling through bracken on the poorly-defined path.

You will eventually reach the old **Dinmor** quarries which are now used to breed fish. Walk along the water's edge until you reach **Trwyn Penmon** opposite **Ynys Seiriol.**

But if the tide is in, you will have to take a different route. Again starting from Benllech, follow the shore to the Ship Inn and around Traeth Coch until you come to a car park. Then along the road to Tywyn. Alternately, you can follow the path inland from Benllech over Castell Mawr to Porthllongdy, and then left down to the Ship Inn and to Tywyn.

Left past the chapel and up the road to the first drive on your left where there is a footpath sign. Left by Pentrellwyn and then right on a track to a stile and on to the National Trust's Bryn Offa estate. From here you can take a footpath to the old quarry mentioned above. From the stile, go right and down by the edge of a field until you reach **Bwrdd Arthur** and to Tan-dinas farm. You will now be able to see Ynys Seiriol.

Follow the farm road to Ty-mawr. Follow the path along the edges of three fields until you come to a disused quarry. Go past it until you reach a road. Walk along this road until you come to a footpath on your left that leads to Ty-cydwys, but before reaching here turn right along a path that takes you past Plas Newydd before turning south which comes back to the road just before the hamlet of Caim. After the houses, the road turns right but keep straight ahead along a road marked No Through Road.

Through the kissing-gate walk alongside a high wall to a stile. Over the stile and right, over another stile and carry on along the path that takes you to **Trwyn Penmon.**

CIRCULAR ROUTE
6 miles – 2 hours
Park near the Owain Glyndŵr pub in Llanddona. Walk towards a sign saying To the beach and walk down the hill. At the junction go to the left and down a steep hill to the shore. Turn right along the road until you come to a car park and Caban y Traeth (a snack bar that is open in summer). You will see a path going to your left onto the beach.

Turn right and walk along the beach to its end. You will then see a coastal path sign and the steps going up a slight slope to your right to a kissing-gate. Then left along the field edge to another kissing-gate. Then follow the footpath up the slope towards a bungalow. Over a stile and through a gate by a cottage and then right up the lane, past some houses.

At the T-junction, go left up a steep hill towards the television mast. There is a beautiful view of Red Wharf Bay and Llanddona beach from here. Up to the mast, and then right at a T-junction. Walk along the road until you come to another junction; bear right here and into Llanddona. Past a housing estate on your right and back to the Owain Glyndŵr pub.

PLACES OF INTEREST

Bwrdd Arthur or Din Silwy: A fortress was built here in pre-Roman times and is defended by eight-foot thick limestone slabs. Third and fourth century pottery and Roman coins have been found here.

Castell Mawr: Stone quarried here was used to build Beaumaris and Caernarfon castles, and later for the construction of the docks and many fine buildings in Liverpool.

Llanddona: In the olden days, Llanddona was renowned for its witches. It is said that a boat, wrecked on Traeth Coch (Red Wharf Bay) in the 16th century carried several red-haired witches who spoke no Welsh. They settled in Llanddona. One, Sian Bwt, was a dwarf with two thumbs on her left hand. The boat arrived – so it is said – oarless and rudderless (it was a custom to put evildoers in such a boat) full of men and women suffering from exposure, hunger and thirst. The women practised witchcraft and begged and frightened the villagers, while their husbands were smugglers who were also said to have magical powers.

On Llanddona beach was an early flying experiment when William Ellis Williams, a physicist, built a monoplane of ash and bamboo. In September 1913 the plane reached 37 miles per hour and reached a height of seven feet.

The church at Llanddona, dedicated to St Dona who probably lived in the 6th century, has a 15th century doorway and was extensively repaired in the 19th century.

Penmon: The quarries of Dinmor in Penmon have supplied stone for many important buildings and developments such as the two bridges across the Menai Strait, the harbour at Caergybi (Holyhead), Birmingham Town Hall and many important buildings in Liverpool. Millstones were also quarried in the vicinity. There was a harbour here for exporting the stone. Some of the quarries have now filled with water and are used for the rearing of fish such as sea bass.

The Vikings attacked Penmon in the latter years of the 10th century and intermittently afterwards while the Normans were in occupation. Another name for Ynys Seiriol is Priestholm, given it by the Vikings.

Traeth Coch (Red Wharf Bay) – is probably named after a Viking invasion in 1170. One battle was particularly bloody and blood ran along the beach which gave it the Welsh name Traeth Coch or red beach. In 1995, a Viking settlement was found near Traeth Coch – the only one on Ynys Môn. There were two large halls as well as evidence of farming, forging and trading there.

It was a very busy port in the 18th and 19th centuries with a small ship-building industry, although there are records of port dues being paid here going back to 1407. Over the centuries there have been many plans to develop the bay. The first was in 1812 when a scheme to build a railway to carry coal from the Pentre Berw mines was devised along with the construction of a quay for coal boats. And the last in 1947, when there was a proposal to build a small pier here.

In 1862, during the American Civil War, a ship called the *Enrica* was built in Birkenhead for a certain Mr Bulloch. Mr Bulloch was a spy for the Confederates and as the Union had heard of his activities, the *USS Tuscarora* was sent to the waters off north Wales. But before the *Tuscarora* arrived, Bullock had sent a crew of Confederate sailors to Moelfre to take charge of the *Enrica* which lay off Traeth Coch. A local man, John Roberts, came across the sailors and he was kidnapped and taken onto the *Enrica*. The Confederate ship, later named the *CSS Alabama*, escaped into the open sea, with John Roberts on board, and during its reign of terror sank 65 ships and cargo, valued at $4,000,000.

Trwyn Penmon: Opposite Ynys Seiriol are old coastguard cottages and an old lifeboat station. The first lifeboat was stationed here in 1831 but was moved to Moelfre in 1848. The present lifeboat house was built in 1880 and was kept here until 1914 when it was moved to Beaumaris. A lighthouse was erected on the island near Trwyn Du after the sinking of the *Rothsay Castle* in 1831 with the loss of nearly 150 crew and passengers. At first the lighthouse was manned by two keepers but in 1922 it became automatic. It was converted to solar power in 1996.

Ynys Seiriol (Puffin Island): The island was named after St Seiriol who founded a religious settlement in Penmon in the 6th century. Seiriol is said to have laid a pavement from Ynys Seiriol to Penmaenmawr on the mainland across what was then marshy ground. He is thought to be buried on the island. The monastic cells are obscured by undergrowth but the 12th century church tower can still be seen from above Trwyn Du. In AD 632, Cadwallon, King of Gwynedd, was besieged here by the Saxon king, Edwin of Northumbria.

There was once a great colony of puffins here. At one time they were caught and pickled and sent in barrels to the cities of England where they were considered a delicacy. This and the ever increasing colony of rats decimated the puffin population. There are still important colonies of cormorants and kittiwakes here.

When the semaphore signalling system between Caergybi (Holyhead) and Liverpool was established in the 19th century, Ynys Seiriol was chosen as a site for one of the stations.

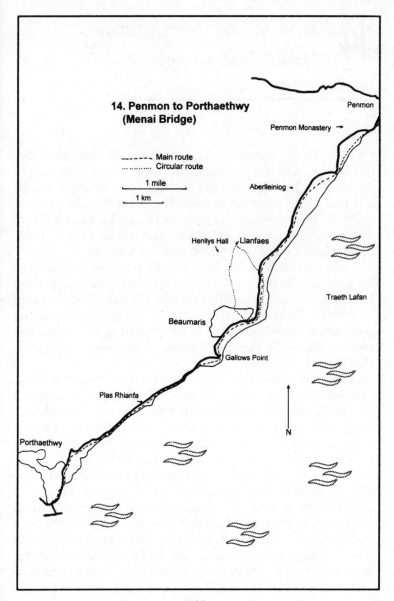

14. Penmon to Porthaethwy
(Menai Bridge)

Penmon

Penmon Monastery →

------- Main route
··········· Circular route

1 mile

1 km

Aberlleiniog →

Henllys Hall ┐ ┌ Llanfaes

Traeth Lafan

Beaumaris

Gallows Point

Plas Rhianfa

N

Porthaethwy

123

14 Penmon to Porthaethwy
(Menai Bridge)

10 miles – 5 hours

From Trwyn Du, opposite the lighthouse, walk along the shore, but at high tide it is impossible to walk this way as the sea comes up to the rock in front of the large white house. Although it is possible to rejoin the shore after passing the cafe, you will reach a headland which you again can't walk past and it is very difficult scrambling up the slope. You would anyway reach private land, covered in bracken and thorn bushes.

Unfortunately you may have to walk along the road as far as the dovecote. To the left just before reaching the dovecote there is a track to your left which takes you to a gate. There is a sign on the gate 'Danger – Quarry workings' but no sign prohibiting you from following the track to the disused quarry. Otherwise you can follow the road past **Penmon monastery** until you are able to reach the shore.

From the quarry buildings you are able to reach the shore. Proceed along the shore past more ruined quarry buildings, a pier and a farm. You will then if the tide is in have to walk for a short while along the road. Then, after a small lay-by, you can rejoin the shore. This is where you will rejoin the shore if you have walked along the road past Penmon monastery.

You might, also, have to walk along the road later on. Then after another lay-by, you can join the shore once again by a public footpath sign. Although signposted Anglesey Coastal Path, parts of this route is difficult if the tide is in. The river that runs to the beach is Afon Lleiniog; upstream are the remains of **Aberlleiniog** castle. To your left is **Traeth Lafan** and the mainland coast and to your left the site of the former Saunders-

Roe factory and **Llanfaes.** On the shore are remains of buildings and slipways belonging to the factory and the old lifeboat station. You may have to walk along the pavement in parts here.

At the end of the pavement you can go down to the shore or follow a clifftop path to Beaumaris. At one time, you could walk along the beach to Beaumaris' sealife centre and then on to the promenade, but since the centre is now closed the only way you can reach the prom, if the tide is in, is along the clifftop path.

Walk along the prom with the castle on your right. The fine building on your right is **Victoria Terrace.** You will then pass the present lifeboat house and pier and along the shore or promenade until you reach a large chimney (the old town baths chimney). You cannot proceed along the shore here and you have to make a short detour into the town; along the main street and back onto the shore until you reach the shipyard at **Gallows Point.**

Go right around the shoreline until you once again reach the main road. The stage from here to Porthaethwy (Menai Bridge) can be quite difficult, scrambling over seaweed covered rocks, and if the tide is in the last bit is impossible. The less adventurous may prefer the narrow winding road without pavement to Porthaethwy.

If walking the shore you will go past the Gazelle Hotel and then towards the Glyn Garth apartment block, where the actor Roger Moore was once reputed to have a flat. It is only possible to go past here at very low tide and even then it is very muddy. Otherwise, after a drink at the Gazelle, go onto the main road and just before **Plas Rhianfa** apartments you will see a public footpath sign to your left taking you back to the shore, but if the tide is in, follow the road into Porthaethwy.

If following the shore, before Ynys y Big you will reach a jetty where it is impossible to follow the shore if the tide is in without going onto private land. If the tide is out you can just about walk through the mud around the jetty. I would strongly suggest taking a partner (and rope!) with you in case you get stuck in the mud.

Proceed along the shore until you reach the outskirts of Porthaethwy. You will walk under the pier leading to Bangor University's research ship with their marine science building on your right. Walk (in the mud) at the bottom of the harbour wall until you come to Porth Daniel where you can make your way to the road by the Liverpool Arms. Bear left past the timber yard towards Porth y Wrach. You can now either return to the shore and scramble over the rocks until you reach a grassy patch or you can continue along the road. You will now have reached Pont y Borth (The Menai Suspension Bridge) and the end of your journey around Ynys Môn. To get back into town, retrace your steps down the road and then left up Ffordd Cambria which will take you to the entrance to the bridge.

CIRCULAR ROUTE
2½ miles – 1 hour

Park your car in Beaumaris and look for Church Street which runs at a right angle from the main street (it's between a butcher and newsagents shop). Up Church Street to a junction where you will see a sign to **Henllys Hall**. *Turn right along the road, eventually passing Baron Hill Estate Lodge on the left. At the driveway to Henllys Hall, turn right down the road and then look for a footpath sign on your left.*

Follow this footpath which follows a fence skirting the edge of a golf course, then right following iron railings to the bottom of the field and into Llanfaes. Right here, down the hill passing the entrance to a derelict factory on your left and down to the main road.

Cross the road onto a pavement on the shore of the Menai Strait and turn right. When you come to the end of the wall, you will see a gap. Through the gap you will see steps. If the tide is out you can walk along the shore or otherwise follow the footpath through a field along the edge of the cliff. Both take you onto Beaumaris promenade. Walk back into town and to your parked car.

PLACES OF INTEREST

Aberlleiniog: During the Norman invasion of 1090, the Earl of Chester built a timber castle on this mound but it was captured by Gruffudd ap Cynan. In the 17th century, a stone fort was built here.

Baron Hill: This derelict mansion was once the home of the Williams-Bulkeley family. William Bulkeley came here from Cheshire in about 1440 to become Constable of Beaumaris Castle. The first mansion was built in 1618, then rebuilt in 1776. Further alterations were made in the 1850s. During the Second World War it was occupied by the Royal Welch Fusiliers and has remained empty since then. At one time, Princess Siwan's (wife of Llywelyn Fawr) coffin was used as a horse watering trough here before it was moved to the parish church. It was the Baron Hill family who paid for the building of the winding road between Beaumaris to Porthaethwy (Menai Bridge) to facilitate travel to the new Menai Bridge.

Beaumaris: Work commenced on the town and castle of Beaumaris in 1295 on marshy ground (beau mareys being 'beautiful marsh' in Norman French). The inhabitants of nearby Llanfaes were evicted to Rhosyr on the west of the island, which became Newborough, in order to build the Norman structures. It was the last of the castles that Edward I built to contain the Welsh. At one time, ships were built at Gallows Point, to the west of the town (so named because this is where prisoners from Beaumaris gaol were hanged), and there was an important fishing industry here. To the east of the town are the remains of an old lifeboat station which was built in 1914.

Opposite the promenade is **Victoria Terrace** designed by Joseph Hansom of Hansom cab fame; the building has by now been converted to apartments. Joseph Hansom also designed Beaumaris gaol and the Bulkeley Arms Hotel.

Henllys Hall – is an imposing building situated in 150 acres of land. There was a building here in the 13th century. At present it is a hotel, but for about 20 years it was a monastery.

Llanfaes – was an important medieval commercial centre and major port. A friary was founded here in 1237 by Llywelyn Fawr in honour of his wife Siwan, daughter of King John of England. When Siwan died her body was carried across Traeth Lafan to the friary. Also buried here were Senena, Llywelyn's mother, and Eleanor de Montford, wife of Llywelyn ap Gruffudd. The cover stone of Siwan's coffin is in Beaumaris Church. Nothing remains of the medieval village or friary and they are probably under the site of a factory built during the Second World War to build Catalina flying boats. During the building of the slipway here, workmen found human bones, believed to be the remains of some of the occupants of the friary. Later the factory built boats and recently refuse lorries; this business has now been transferred to a new factory in Llangefni.

At one time, ferries transported people from Llanfaes to the mainland. The service was later transferred to The Green at Beaumaris.

Penmon monastery: After the Normans abandoned the area, the Welsh princes seized back their lands. This was the period when the monastery at Penmon was built. When Llywelyn Fawr became prince, he granted Penmon to the Prior and Canons of Ynys Seiriol and it was during this period – the 12th century – that the monastic buildings were built. Although many of the buildings are ruined, the church is still in use. Near the church is a dovecote from the 1600s.

Plas Rhianfa – an old mansion now converted into holiday flats. It is reputed that many refugees from the Hungarian Uprising – including the famous footballer Puskas – stayed here for a few months after arriving in a furniture van!

Traeth Lafan (Lavan Sands): The crossing of the sands is only safe for three or four hours in every twelve. Old charts show two routes, one below Penmaenmawr and another further west. Travellers had to walk for four miles over the sands to meet the Beaumaris ferry. Those going in opposite direction, were left on the sands, often in total darkness and were guided to the mainland by a tolling bell. It is still possible to cross the sands today – apart from the channel, but only with an experienced guide. A duel was fought on these sands in the 17th century between Colonel Bulkeley of the nearby Baron Hill mansion who had led Royalist forces during the Civil War and Thomas Cheadle, a traitor who had worked for and later married into the family. Bulkeley was killed and Cheadle was hanged at Conwy.

INDUSTRIAL, AVIATION & RAILWAY HERITAGE
FROM
GWASG CARREG GWALCH

- **SLATE QUARRYING IN WALES**
  - Alun John Richards. From its earliest beginnings to the present day, this book follows the fortunes and misfortunes of this great industry. 231 pp. *ISBN 0-86381-319-4; £7.50*

- **SLATE QUARRYING IN CORRIS**
  - Alun John Richards. First detailed account of the area. 144 pp. *ISBN 0-86381-279-1; £5.45*

- **DELVING IN DINORWIG**
  - Douglas C. Carrington. First detailed account of a fascinating slate quarry. *ISBN 0-86381-285-6; £7.50*

- **THE GOLDEN AGE OF BRYMBO STEAM**
  - Geoff and Hugh Charles. Old photographs and memories of the Brymbo railway lines. *ISBN 0-86381-435-2; £5.75*

- **THREE STOPS TO THE SUMMIT**
  - Rol Willams. The History of the Snowdon Mountain Railway. *ISBN 0-86381-433-6; £4.95*

- **HISTORIC LANDSCAPES OF THE GREAT ORME**
  - Mary Aris. Early agriculture and copper-mining - a new perspective on Llandudno's landscape and history. 114 pages quarto; maps; diagrams; illustrations. *ISBN 0-86381-357-7; £7.95*

- **THE LLŶN PENINSULA MINES**
  - Wil Williams. A history of manganese mining on the peninsula; 64 pages; bilingual; illustrations. *ISBN 0-86381-315-1; £3*

- **THE SLATE QUARRIES OF PEMBROKESHIRE**
  - Alun John Richards. Including illustrations & maps. *ISBN 0-86381-484-0; £5.50*

- **EARLY AVIATION IN NORTH WALES**
  - Roy Sloan. From early nineteenth century balloon flights to the outbreak of World War II. 168 pp. *ISBN 0-86381-119-1; £2.75*

- **WINGS OF WAR OVER GWYNEDD**
  - Roy Sloan. Aviation in Gwynedd during World War II. 200 pp. *ISBN 0-86381-189-2; £4.50*

- **AIRCRAFT CRASHES IN GWYNEDD**
  - Roy Sloan. Flying accidents in Gwynedd 1910-1990. 168 pp. *ISBN 0-86381-281-3; £5.50*

- **DOWN IN WALES**
  - Terence R. Hill. Visits to some war-time air crash sites. 94 quarto pp. *ISBN 0-86381-283-X; £6.50*